The Icon in
my Pocket

We gotta go, and never will stop till we get there.
Where are we going, man?
I don't know, but we gotta go.
Jack Kerouac

Why are you surprised that your journeys do not help you
when you have yourself with you? You are pursued by the
same worries which forced you on your way.
What enjoyment can new countries give you? Or knowledge of other towns and places? Your restlessness has not
taken you anywhere.
Seneca

I long for the land that is not, for everything that is I am
weary of craving.
Edith Södergran

To Sara

The Icon in my Pocket

Owe Wikström

*Translated into English
by Yvonne King*

GRACEWING

This work was first published in Swedish in 2004
under the title
Ikonen i Fickan
by Bokförlaget Natur och Kultur
Karlavägen 31, PO Box 27 323
S – 102 54 Stockholm, Sweden

First published in English in 2008 by
Gracewing
2 Southern Avenue, Leominster
Herefordshire HR6 0QF

ISBN 978 0 85244 667 6

Typesetting by Action Publishing Technology Ltd,
Gloucester, GL1 5SR

CONTENTS

INTRODUCTION

The snow that fell a couple of days ago has practically disappeared. I can sense that winter is on its way out. But there are still no birds in the sky. The town is foggy and depressing. The snow is slightly grey and is melting in trickles along the streets. Only a few weeks ago icy winds were blowing and people stood huddled in dark bus shelters waiting for the journey into town. Now there is a pale watery sunlight. People's pasty faces can be clearly seen. The sun: where is the sun?

For a couple of weeks I have rooted around among my papers, made a great many telephone calls, stood for hours by the bookcase, looked through old waxed paper books, sat at the computer and searched for files on the hard disc. I have packed windproof khaki trousers, sunglasses and pens. Finally I make my way down to Stockholm Central Station. The snow has started to melt and the wheels of my heavy case leave wide tracks as I drag it along behind me. It is full of books on *flâneurs,* pilgrims, tourists and backpackers. There are notes and articles on icons; research on leisure; and on Russian and Spanish mystics, and some CDs in a case. I have even brought along my old work companion – my wafer-thin laptop. In it I keep drafts and notes. Observations and unfinished trains of thought float about in the hard disc's dark memory. The batteries are new. I can avoid the hassle of cables and can write – for hours – wherever I am. A period of writing is looming. I fling my bag up

onto the overhead rack and lean backwards. In my pocket
is a little Russian icon.

Before the train leaves I look out over Stockholm Central
Station. Some people are dragging their luggage along the
platforms whilst others are staring at information boards.
Someone is obviously late and rushes past with their keys
rattling in their jacket pocket. Others doze on a bench
whilst waiting for their connections. A young woman is
leaning against a wall. She has green hair and extremely
pointed shoes. With a glazed look and eyes staring into the
distance she is on an inward journey listening to music
through her earphones. She is on a different kind of
journey. She is swaying, very slightly, in time to the music.

And so the train struggles on its way. We pass rows of
grey buildings and houses that look like crumpled milk
cartons in their garish colours; a kind of visual pollution.
The flat industrial landscape glides past. It is not a pretty
sight. The train picks up speed. I am travelling in a 'Quiet
Carriage' – no mobile phones are allowed.

The carriage is soon transformed into a moving meditation chamber. The train's relaxing vibrations and the
carriage's enclosed space create a bubble of time and space.
Some of the passengers are staring at their diaries deep in
thought. Others are dozing. Many are reading paperbacks
or crumpled copies of *Metro*. At best the train offers a loose
sort of community feeling, no shrill voices and no enforced
intimacy. Someone is sending SMS messages. The early
spring light is restful. Whilst we are separate from one
another, we are also taking part in a communal journey.
Long train journeys are restful for the soul. Perhaps it is the
rocking motion that does it. But today the loudspeaker
intrudes all too quickly. 'Next stop: Arlanda Airport.'

In common with so many others I like to travel out into
the world, preferably to Europe, but also to other continents. For good or ill I have travelled a great deal during my
career. Perhaps I travel to become acquainted with new and
unknown environments, discover life stories behind chance
encounters, experience smells, foreign foods, history,

customs and views. The blue waters of the Mediterranean, bougainvillea and cypresses against chalk-white houses as well as the south's mild brown-black nights may be hackneyed images – but is there anything better for a washed-out Scandinavian? When the cloudy grey days of winter begin to increase I seek contrasts. The pavement cafés in large cities are just as tempting to me as anonymous small towns in the former eastern bloc countries. On the other hand – is there anything more beautiful than Swedish summers or the wildness of the Norwegian mountains?

In recent years I have become more interested in consequences – both social and spiritual – of mobility, this constant movement. Travel can be used as a *metaphor* for a person's way of interacting with society. As a cliché one could say that some act like drifters – they take each day as it comes. Others are forever seeking new challenges, they are chasing the exotic – a sort of existential backpacker. Many prefer instead to live safely. As package tourists they travel calmly through life. Their outings are regulated and cushioned. Others are cultural tourists – they ceaselessly read books and go to the theatre, all in order to enrich their inner lives. Some are pilgrims – en route to an unseen reality. The narrative of the journey can itself be seen as an identity marker: 'I never travel by charter! Yuk, all those people!' some say with aversion. Others love group travel and crowded camp sites as much as the smell of barbecues or the communal strolling of mini-golfers. To talk about your dream travel destination or where you would *not* wish to travel says something about who you are.

I am particularly fascinated by two opposite poles in the 'psychology of travel'; on the one hand the hunt for the ultimate experience and on the other hand the melancholy feelings that travel gives rise to. Both of these overlap with the inward journey; man's search for *something more*, something more elevated than the chalk-white sandy beaches or the charm of pavement cafés, something apart from the cultural highs and the scaling of inaccessible mountains.

For a long time there has been a certain embarrassment

in Sweden about discussing spiritual questions. Perhaps it is now time to let go. In my work – on the borders of psychology and religion – I am more and more meeting a genuine questioning. As the evening progresses many conversations lead on to existential emptiness; the search for meaning. Disillusioned after far too many tips on how to become happier – by positive thinking or by reading deep meaningful books – so many people many people seem to be looking around for a deeper sense of belonging.

The need for seriousness is often palpable in an all too ironic generation, but many people lack the words to express these feelings and feel lost.

Another – more private – reason for my interest in travel is that, paradoxically enough, I find it easiest to concentrate and write in an anonymous environment, in cheap hotel rooms in half-forgotten places. Impersonal furnishings, where there are no personal objects, as well as clapped-out sofas and tatty shelves from the 1950s, have a calming and stimulating effect. Most of all I prefer dark window tables in cafés, restaurants or waiting rooms. It is not the fashionable that I am seeking but the undemanding. Calmness radiates from the chink of crockery, small talk and snatches of laughter from several tables away. It is life-enhancing and deeply creative. No music in the background. My area of research – the psychology of religion – is not intended to be about outward journeys, even if pilgrimages can be seen as a symbiosis of outer and inner journeys, but a single individual's *inner journey*, irrespective of where they are situated geographically. For example, people make an inner journey when they retreat into 'another world' when reading a novel; then they are visiting an epic universe. Part of my research has been devoted to trying to understand the 'reality' that readers find themselves in when they associate with the character in a novel or when a person realizes that someone is listening to their prayers. I have particularly tried to understand a special type of inner journey – one which is sometimes called existential or spiritual. Such a journey touches on the process which often starts when a person gradually or abruptly is forced to ask themselves questions about the meaning of life, the brutality of death and the possibility of a divine reality.

Such journeys begin when meeting life crises, when weary of the world or anxious about life's transience. This often begins when a person enters into the second half of their life and with a certain melancholy asks themselves, 'Is that all that there is to life? How quickly it has all passed.' Such reflections often lead to a subconscious desire to put the brakes on in order to take a new compass bearing and then set off again – but this time to find values that are more lasting. To their surprise the person discovers a new and spiritual side to themselves during this stock taking – a side which hitherto they have considered to be pure childishness and therefore completely ignored.

When someone has reached a long-awaited rest period – whether it be during a holiday's indolent relaxation, or at home – these types of inner journeys often commence. But sometimes too in the middle of a large party with friends, amid laughter and cries of joy a completely different voice can make itself heard – a sense of futility. There are various names for this feeling. It can be called world weariness, existential anxiety, a longing for – why not? – a journey into one's inner self.

This book constitutes a personal attempt to combine various travel interests: those which apply to the *outward*, geographical, the *socially* ideological and the *inner* spiritual journey. I have chosen an essay form which blends obser-vations and arguments with descriptions of local scenes and atmosphere. Elsewhere I have presented the scientific attempt to understand the 'inner journey' (a slightly more elastic expression than the word 'spiritual') as well as its philosophical and psychological preconditions.

Readers can steer their own course through the book. The first part is descriptive and about society in general, whilst the second half is more personal. In the first part I have progressed from being an observer during my travels to becoming more drawn into the religious theme. Towards the end I enter into a serious discussion of Christian mysticism.

But the reader can benefit from reading snippets here and there. Anyone who wishes for more research can go deeper into the bibliography at the end of the book. The book has a logical structure. This can be completely ignored. Now and then the reader is advised to skip certain sections perhaps to return to them later. Why should all books be read from start to finish?

In common with my previous books, this book has evolved during journeys or in the pauses which sometimes arise during my academic work. The final attempt to create some order from piles of notes has partly taken place in a boathouse up on the edge of the Norrland sea coast, two metres above the waves and partly next to a window on the third floor of the Pensione Gargagno with a view eastwards over Lake Garda, Italy.

O.W.
Uppsala

PART I

THE OUTWARD JOURNEY

Think what it must be like to just pack up and go!

Most people say that if they suddenly had a lot of money to spend as they wished, then they would like a change of environment for a while. Nearly everyone puts 'to be able to travel' at the top of the list. The reasons can vary. Some may want a change; to escape from their everyday lives, to get some sunshine or to recharge their batteries. Others want to discover new things about themselves. Some want to travel to be able to take it easy without a guilty conscience, to play golf or to celebrate an important event. Young people throw themselves over the steep waterfalls of extreme sports.

The advertisements shriek out at us: travel brochures are as heavy as lead when they fall through our letter boxes. Travel sections in the daily papers are becoming more and more frequent. Pictures of calm beaches in Asia, yellow taxis in New York or striped deck chairs in resorts on the Black Sea or in the Seychelles flash onto the Internet. In the bookshops there are shelves full of maps and books with tips on everything from restaurants to beautiful views. TV programmes such as Airport are just as popular as travel programmes which promote new destinations.

And we are travelling as never before. Families with children pack sun screen and toys into sports bags. A few hours after they have left their houses, locked the doors and asked the neighbour to water the plants, the parents are sitting on white plastic chairs next to a clear blue swimming pool while the children collect pretty stones on a Mediterranean beach. Business travellers queue at departure gates together with young backpackers with the obligatory bottles of water. And business travel is on the increase. Many academics and business people are impossible to get hold of because they are more often than not 'on a course' or conference usually somewhere in Europe or some other place in the world.

Young people in cut-off jeans, dyed blondes of a 'certain age' out for a good time, reminiscent of the 'Golden Girls' of the American 1980s TV series, and elderly men in shorts lean back in aircraft seats. Enclosed in giant steel tubes they take off from runways around the world, twenty-four hours a day. Some of the passengers are drinking coffee inside silent and barely discernible white streaks several kilometres up in the blue sky. Others are dozing whilst waiting to disembark on another continent.

Every school class with any self-respect goes on a trip together before they go their separate ways after their exams. More than half the population of Sweden has visited either London or Paris. Time zones are crossed more and more frequently and geographical distance is minimized. *The dream* of travelling seems to be constant, and just as important as the trip itself. It is now possible to go on a one-day charter trip to Rome and visit the Piazza Navona, St Peter's Basilica and buy a scarf in the Via dei Condotti – all before evening. *La Città eternal* – the eternal city – in one day! New budget airlines pop up while others go under. The travel industry is one of the world's most lucrative industries despite the terrorist attacks of recent years. The leisure industry is the largest supplier of experiences nowadays.

But there is a downside to the image of the happy traveller. Some of them discover – when they have finally saved enough money to make a once-in-a-lifetime trip to distant continents, set off and relaxed in some far flung place – that in actual fact they really miss home. It is only when they have taken off and realized their dreams that they value their own world: the Swedish sense of order, the Swedish countryside on a summer night, family and friends. Nearly everyone idealizes their travels. The sad solitary moments on a beach, a shabby hotel room in a town where they are practically consumed by homesickness – these things are easily forgotten. The melancholy of travel is overlooked.

Just as important as the actual trip is the recording of it. Photograph albums are squeezed between rows of video cassettes and DVDs on shelves behind the living room sofa. Some can search through their own catalogue of memories via large files of photographs, yellowing entrance tickets that they have saved or serviettes from cafés in Caracas, Bombay or Trondheim which have long since disappeared. Shame-faced and jealous friends look at their more organized friends' travel albums. In their own houses are piles of unsorted photos. Now and then they try to put them into some sort of order, but because they cannot remember where and when they took the various pictures, they soon lose interest. Sometimes they dive into the pile of shoe boxes in the loft but always come down disappointed. Others show their superiority by exclaiming: 'Photos! It would never occur to me to take photos when I travel. You shouldn't try to capture reality!' This is another way of pointing out their own obvious originality.

A great many people have, in a few years, saved thousands of holiday photos onto their hard discs. They send them as attachments with their emails to friends who look at them with marginal interest. On a mobile telephone's minute display we stare in amazement at photos of our friends enjoying the heat down under in New Zealand whilst we are standing freezing outside a department store in the town's pedestrian precincts.

The North/ South Divide

But let us not fool ourselves. Hundreds of thousands of Swedes cannot afford foreign travel. The opportunity to travel is extremely unevenly distributed throughout the world. Society's elite from the world's richer nations have a virtually unfettered access to space, but their time is more restricted. For the masses in the Third World it is exactly the opposite; they have oceans of time but no access to space. Movement is therefore deeply polarized. The rich become more globalized whilst the poor remain more locally tied.

New destinations are idealized and mythologized. Along with this goes exploitation. The travel brochures of the West create a stereotypical picture of the Orient or sub-Saharan Africa which is treacherously over-simplified. They build up prejudices which last for decades, not least the idea of the Orient as a place of strong feelings and wild romance.

Moreover, the entire travel industry contains a dark and cynical streak: the rampant increase in the sex industry. But moral outrage does nothing to reduce the effect of middle-aged erotic under-nourishment or the consequences of commercial power. Well-nourished bronzed broiler youths from rich countries travel without any great embarrassment – around the planet. The cost of one week's charter holiday, drinking beer and diving in a lagoon, or for several months' back-packing in Asia or Latin America ('We're off – it's really cool and dirt cheap'), is the equivalent of years of hard graft on plantations or monotonous cleaning jobs in tourist hotels for the local population. Low budget travellers from the countries in the North work hard for several months in order to create long and indolent free time – for themselves – on trips to the countries of the South. Of course this is an enriching experience as it has always been. Soon they will travel on to new destinations while the local populations of the South pick up their litter and clean the toilets whilst they are on their way back to the airport.

I am even embarrassed to write this myself as I am also part of this unequal distribution of wealth. It does not only apply to the young. From one perspective one can see young people's travel behaviour as an attempt by their generation to put off adulthood, the daily grind and any form of responsibility. By whatever means they can they want to avoid making important decisions about their lives which would mean that they might risk having to settle down and in so doing to lose something. Perhaps they want to take their pensions early. Adulthood terrifies them. From another perspective it could be interpreted as the younger generation's protest against their own parents' workaholic lives: 'They have never allowed themselves to live – they have always been stressed!' The significance of work for one's identity and self-confidence is decreasing. It can even be seen as the twentieth century's equivalent of the Grand Tour. This could also last for years but then as now was reserved for the children of the middle classes.

At the same time, the exotic has become more difficult to reach. Soon every nook and cranny of the earth's surface will have its own web page. Everywhere is accessible by internet. When one travels abroad one has already been there, if only via the world wide web. Nothing seems novel for more than a few weeks. Anything strange soon becomes familiar and quickly enough, banal. On the other hand the exotic becomes more alluring the harder it is to achieve. The world is shrinking.

Summary
The jet streams from tens of thousands of aeroplanes are woven together like a giant cocoon. It lies like a membrane several kilometres above the earth. On board are the twentieth century's travellers: backpackers, cultural tourists, drifters, pilgrims and ordinary tourists among others. More than ever the idea of *homo viator* (the travelling man) becomes a reality. More and more people seem to be on their way, always on their way but where to and why?

Chapter One

THE ALLURE OF TRAVEL

To the Canary Islands! On the longing for sun, sea and sand

Arlanda airport Stockholm – it is still early morning. I am on my way to one of the most popular travel destinations – particularly for those who, like me, feel drawn towards the sun and moderate heat. The Canary Islands, this severely exploited group of islands without any history, in the middle of the Atlantic nothingness. But the weather there is perfect – mild winds and a permanent blue sky.

Before I get onto the plane – today it is a charter flight – I notice a giggling group of people. They start drinking in the departure hall. They are obviously going on a trip to celebrate someone's fiftieth birthday. A younger man orders a large strong beer. Outside there is a cold wind and it is foggy, but they can already feel the rays of the sun. In their bags they have packed swimwear and sun tan oil. When they have gone through passport control they seem to have stepped over a mental threshold. Now they are allowed to be indolent. When we have checked in and the hand baggage has passed through the X-ray machine, many go on board with their boarding passes in their shirt pockets – others are clutching them in their hands.

Some passengers are calmly reading the morning papers. In the airport shop which smells strongly of perfume, men with tired faces are looking at rows of 'toys for boys', browsing through piles of CDs and DVDs and shining electric whisks for caffe latte. In the restaurants several years ago there would have been an obligatory ash tray placed on the table. Now there are mobile phones instead. With blank looks the passengers stare out towards a noisy crowd. And I think to myself: what are we travelling *towards* and what are we travelling *from*?

There are many reasons for trips abroad. Many are probably made because the travellers wish to relax, sleep, sunbathe, eat and drink well, or sit outside on warm nights, meet new people, or play golf. Others travel to visit relatives or old friends in Europe. They travel to Fuertaventura to wind surf, to Vietnam in order to understand the country's modern war history, or to Sydney to study.

One reason for the popularity of package holidays is probably the longed-for laziness, allowing oneself to do nothing, to be able just to stroll along a beach or lie on a sunbed for several hours. Many middle-aged and elderly Swedes appear to have a guilty conscience about anything that smacks of indolence. Because there is a feeling that Swedes 'have Luther on their shoulders', (which is extremely unjust to that theological lover of life), it means that their enjoyment of life and their ability to enjoy themselves on an everyday basis is limited. Perhaps they long for a parenthesis, to be able to read a novel in the middle of the day and for a short time to feel no sense of responsibility – let the hours just pass lazily.

Sometimes one hears: 'Now I am going to "just be".' Travelling away gives a sense of freedom. When we get out into the big wide world we can become anonymous, we avoid being noticed. It is as if we are looking for simplicity, to be finally here *and now* in an existential sense.

Perhaps only a charter ticket can allow us to do this. We are treated like children – others take the responsibility – we can leave all the practical arrangements to them. This regressive pull is as tempting for some as it is threatening for others. Some people talk contemptuously about the package tourist as *turistus vulgaris*. Others fit without difficulty into the standardized package mould. For yet others

the package holiday offers a way of being able to shut themselves within their own shells, but within a group and not
take part, to ignore outings but just to wander round in the
sun by themselves. Quite simply to be left in peace – but in
the company of other people about whom they don't have
to worry.

Package tours

Long before departure time there is a queue at the departure
gate. Many people become irritated when they hear that the
flight is going to be delayed. The company talks about a
'late incoming flight'. So I wander around again for a while
among the airport's shops and cafés. I look around me.
Some people are doing crosswords; others are standing in
corners talking into their mobiles. Some seem to be doing
business whilst staring down at their laptop's email inbox.
Some call and say farewell to friends. But the farewell is
seldom heart-rending. In a few hours they will be able to
talk to each other again from the far away hotel's chalk-
white balconies or go into some Internet café in the warm
south.

We are a motley crew: students going on an exchange
year, I who want to write, even more who want to
sunbathe. A little way off I can see the backpackers sitting
on the ground, an older couple who have checked in for Rio
de Janiero and a boy with a label round his neck is taken by
the airport staff to the gate for the flight to New York.

I read in a book that the first English charter aircraft
landed on Corsica in 1949. It was not until the sixties that
group travel started to interest a larger number of English,
German and Scandinavian tourists. The Italian Mediterranean coast was the place on to which the Northern Europeans projected all of their sun-starved fantasies. And this
ideal has certainly not lessened.

The concept of the charms of the Mediterranean has its
roots in the cultural travel of the eighteenth century and
more recently has been watered down by the hordes of

Northern Europeans who – like me – love to bathe in the azure blue waves. In those days it was considered obligatory to stay in cities such as Rome or Padua. Art treasures had to be viewed. Authors travelled round and wrote comprehensive travelogues. The books were later read by northerners longing for some warmth whilst the snow whistled round the doorsteps. The author Stendhal is said to have suffered from a nervous breakdown when he arrived in Florence; there were far too many artistic impressions for this sensitive artist. Our own August Strindberg was much more prosaic. He thought that the Palatine in Rome looked more like a pile of rubbish than anything else and quickly walked away. A long time later some of them began depicting the Mediterranean in a more romantic light, such as Göran Schildt in his travels with the boat *Daphne*. In *The Sun Boat* from 1956 he fascinated his readers with his diary from a sailing voyage around the coast of Greece, towards Egypt and then along the Nile. His description of the lapping of the bow wave and the dark nights still exists in the northern European perception of the good life.

During the early fifties it was first the French and then the Italian Riviera that were the 'in' places. That's where the hedonistic life was to be found. Actors with well-known names such as Jean Paul Belmondo and Brigitte Bardot have given a permanent lustre to the palms, the stone houses glowing in the twilight and the din of the waves. Place names such as Menton, Nice or Marseille have been familiar to northerners for decades.

∾⊖∾

It was Thomas Cook (1808–1892) who was responsible for the *Mediterraneanization* of the European leisure culture. Group travel was organized as early as the end of the nineteenth century using his travel guides as examples. When the railways had been laid through Europe, Cook offered train journeys down through the Continent; breakfast in London, and dinner in Nice the following day. The good life became associated with various cultural personalities. They also set up home on the coast, artists such as Fernand Leger and Picasso or authors such as John Dos Passos.

As soon as group travel increased it became a luxury which was soon available for northern Europeans on quite ordinary salaries. The fashionable became accessible because it was converted into a commodity which could be purchased. Then sunbathing was packaged and sold, something which previously had only been known in Scandinavia and Germany. But as soon as tour buses discharged hordes of sun-starved northern Europeans, the Bohemian intellectuals slipped away.

But the *italianization* of the world had begun. Many people had developed an idealized picture of nature which would colour much of northern Europe's permanent yearning: 'I am longing for Italy, for Italy's beautiful land, where small yellow lemons, grow along the shore,' sang the popular Swedish song-writer Birger Sjöberg in the 1960s.

And then I think that perhaps this is what we are travelling *towards; La Dolce Vita*. Palm trees, the salty tang of the sea, seaweed and beaches are perhaps the paradise that we are longing for. The Mediterranean area has become for Europeans just as much a symbol of happiness and *leisure time* as Florida has for Americans.

The increase in frequent travel

But on this occasion my trip is not to the Mediterranean but to *Gran Canaria* – the most popular holiday destination for Swedes. We all stand obediently in a queue. Sweaty children are fighting in their parents' arms; an elderly couple pat a boy on the head. It takes an unbearably long time to pass through ticket control. Then the queue wends its way into the long belly of the plane. There is quiet background music playing and the cabin crew with permanently fixed smiles pass out forms for something or other. An experienced business traveller, who has obviously been more or less forced by his wife to go on this trip, complains that people are so 'awkward'. I can hear as he hisses out of the corner of his mouth that they don't even know what a *gate* is, and that some of them are delaying the whole of the boarding process by slowly placing their hand baggage in the overhead lockers and don't give a damn about the people waiting behind them. His irritation is tangible. His face is still bright red long after everyone else has settled down in their seats.

An elderly woman carefully puts ear plugs in. She gets out a book that appears to be new. She will read throughout the entire five-hour flight. Some small children crawl around in the gangways. Eventually everyone is in their place: 'Boarding completed!'

When the captain informs us that there will be a further few minutes' delay the irritated man starts writhing about in his seat. The lady with the ear plugs ignores the whole thing. She carries on calmly reading. Then the murmuring starts. Most of the passengers bury their heads in the inflight magazines advertising perfume and duty-free goods. If we order them now they will be ready and waiting in plastic bags on our seats when we board the plane for the return flight in one or two weeks' time. I look out through the minute window. Arlanda airport is grey and cold looking. We are still parked on the apron. Slowly like giant insects the planes move out onto the runway. Some land, others are in the queue in front of us.

Then the sound of the engines increases and the plane moves slowly, swaying slightly, towards the runway. Finally the sound of the engines goes from a vague whine to a long drawn-out roar. We are sitting wedged in with barely enough room for our knees. The pilot lets out the throttle. We are pressed backwards by the acceleration. The plane sways, drags itself up into the sky and the landing gear is retracted.

Soon there is only space, cold and infinite only half a metre from my elbow. Only a membrane of glass separates me from the air outside. We are all sitting stuffed into this metal tube; nearly three hundred sun-starved travellers.

Slowly we climb through the milk-white fog – outside I suddenly see the intense, clear blue sky. Swaying, the plane drags itself even higher into the atmosphere as if from a padded quilt. The cabin crew push their heavy food trolleys along the gangway. After only half an hour it is practically ten kilometres down to the ground and our speed is nearly a thousand kilometres an hour.

Even ten years ago the passengers would be staring wide-eyed down at the ground as the plane took off. They would be observing their slow passage up over the earth in wonder. A long distance under the wings the ground seems to move at ultra rapid speed. Even earlier, at the dawn of passenger flight, many of the passengers would stand up on the narrow seats and take photos of the towns or the snowy tops of the Alps as they flew over them. Now most of it is just routine. Few even bother to look at the view. Beneath the plane lies grey Sweden in late winter. Up here we encounter blinding sunshine with cloud formations that look like the Himalayas.

We can hear the drone of the engines. There is a cold draught in our faces. Many passengers are reading the daily papers. Soon we will be eating tepid food, chatting with our fellow passengers or snoozing for a while. After several hours we will disembark in another landscape, on another continent.

Travel's stereotypes

The plane is now in the correct lane in the motorway in the sky. We are rocked gently south across Europe. Some of the passengers are dozing with their chins on their chests, others read the in-flight magazines, listen to music, test perfumes or take a drink. There is a pleasant, cool and slightly damp flow of air from the air conditioning. The din in the cabin dies down. Below on the ground it is possible to make out lakes and towns. You can see an *autostrada*. Buses are slowly creeping south.

When group travel started in earnest after the Second

World War it was buses that were first off the mark. They were cheap and had room for a lot of passengers. The North Italian beaches – especially Rimini, south of Ravenna – were the first destinations. The long journey down to the Mediterranean and also to the flowers of Mainau or the Passion Play in Oberammergau, meant that the bus became one's own 'home' throughout the journey. Everyone had their own place in the bus. The only familiar thing in an unfamiliar world was one's own seat which one marked with a book or a jumper placed on the seat. The consciousness of belonging to a group became apparent. The size of the bus dictated the size of the group. Not so large that it created anonymity, but at the same time small enough so that the individual could not become inconspicuous for a couple of hours. The group dynamic was maintained by singing songs or someone telling funny stories. There was a warm enjoyment during bus tours which lasted until the passengers arrived at their famous beach or castle destination. Friendships were made and reinforced. A whole generation has photo albums full of such holiday memories.

But that was fifty years ago. Nowadays bus passengers are either pensioners – usually a group interested in visiting castles or on music or other cultural holidays – or young people. Entire school classes hire buses to get cheaply and easily to the ski resorts in the Alps.

When flying became cheaper stereotypical charter passengers quickly evolved. These stereotypes still exist. They have been depicted in films such as Lasse Åberg's *Package Holiday*. In this film we see a wonderful old couple on their first foreign holiday, nervous about the check-in and with their tickets always held ready. There is the engineer – a keen photographer – with his bored wife; the newly weds with eyes only for each other; the man who always complains about everything; the woman who only has eyes for the handsome Spaniards; and a couple of bachelors who were drunk from check-in to arrival back at Arlanda Airport.

I look around me at the other passengers on the plane

and of course these stereotypes are all still here. Three rows behind me I see the happy couple who are at last on their way and are now clinging to each other. There are some young people asleep with open mouths – others are already merry. Children are rushing up and down the aisles. The elderly woman continues to read calmly.

In Europe we had the longest holidays in the world straight after the war. In contrast to workers in the USA, European workers took their benefits in holidays rather than in pay. Because of this a complete leisure market arose which quickly expanded.

Mallorca was the preferred destination during the sixties. This boom created a moral debate in Sweden. The newspapers wrote that most people seemed to lose their inhibitions as soon as they fastened their seatbelts in the DC3. Anything could happen: men and women drank and sinned. Drunken men and shameless women crawled round the bars in the Mediterranean. An Annika fell in love with an Alfredo who as soon as Annika had gone home would pick up the next love-starved woman. This was the image of hedonism in 1962, but according to Orvar Löfgren in his book *On vacationing*, it was most probably a construction of the mass media. A similar discussion has taken place since the beginning of the twenty-first century. Teenagers stagger around the bars in Greece while the local residents have to clean up the vomit left by spoilt northern Europeans – all according to the evening papers.

Year after year there has been a gradual increase in package holiday makers from Europe. From 6 million in 1960, 30 million in 1975 to 70 million in 2000. In the seventies the destinations included Spain, the Canary Islands and the Greek Islands. When jet planes came into service travellers could take themselves to warmer climes even faster than before. The aircraft companies had an overcapacity of seats. Because the Canary Islands became the new destination, it meant that summer was only five hours away and so the holiday season could be stretched over the entire year. Out in the Atlantic in the middle of nowhere, were several volcanic islands with the most important thing of all: a stable but not too extreme summer climate – day in and day out. Now there is competition from Egypt's artificial tourist paradise, not to mention Thailand.

Ever since autumn I have been looking though the travel brochures, and causing some raised eyebrows among people who consider the Canary Islands as the lowest form of destination. To sit sweating in hot buses or planes that are full to bursting does not appeal to the sensibilities of the middle classes. In several hours the extinct volcano Tejde will appear on the right. After that the plane will make several steep turns, and then we will be on the ground. But there are still a couple of hours left. There is still a cool breeze from the air conditioning.

Luxury for sale

Our meals are placed on the minute meal trays. The quantity of plastic wrapping means that I can barely make out what sort of food it is. My elbow is in my neighbour's butter packet. There is a plastic membrane around the cheese. Desperately I try to make a tear in it but am having no luck despite trying to rip it open with my teeth. 'Would you like cognac with your coffee?' – 'Yes, please!' A feeling of sophistication at this hour of the morning as the captain announces that we can see Paris down below to the left.

One of the pilots comes out into the aisle. When I see his dazzling white shirt and the gleaming gold buttons I think of how a uniform's severity exudes ostentation and luxury. The strict dress code of the pilot and the cabin crew contrast in their elegance with the passengers' pastel coloured track suits, colourful shirts and well-worn Birkenstocks. This is somewhat different from the business travellers' smart suits, brown Italian shoes and pale skin, those who relax back in first class and talk on their telephones until the doors are closed and the plane screeches on its way.

But this is luxury for the mass market. It has a long history going back to the cruise ships. Around the turn of the twentieth century the shipping lines competed to create the most luxurious ocean going liners with even bigger first-class decks with palm trees in greenhouses, swimming pools and lounges. The Americans built the giant liner *Oceanic*, the English had their *Titanic*, the Germans their *Imperator* and the French *France*. Around these giant vessels were regular departures and arrivals with champagne and fruit baskets. This ritualized luxury even contained an erotic and glossy picture of life on board: 'Never a dull moment!'

These luxurious packaged voyages with ocean steamers are the forerunners of the package cruises with inclusive harbour visits which are increasing during the beginning of the twenty-first century. They are found in the cruises around the Bahamas off the coast of Florida or cruises to the Mediterranean. The American liner *Voyager of the Seas* which was launched in 1999 can accommodate 3,100 passengers and has 1,200 crew members, golf courses, basket ball courts, an ice rink, climbing walls, jogging tracks, bars and restaurants.

Today's northern European ferry industry such as the Finland ferries had a low status image for a time. One way of erasing this was to align itself to the inter-war period's luxurious travel culture. Even car ferries between the Nordic countries or to the Continent are profiting from the demand for luxury. For just a few short hours during a night sailing across the Baltic or North Sea many people can enjoy the good life.

But back to the pilot. The stylish sailors' uniforms – the charisma was captured in the popular long running Swedish TV series *Rederiet* (*The Shipping Line*) – were eventually adopted by the airlines' sun-tanned captains. There are obvious marks of rank, white shirts and tightly buttoned jackets. Even the cabin crew's black gloves were a sign of fashion in the infancy of passenger flight. The entire flight has a clear semiotic which is intended to give the appearance of safety.

During recent years the cabin crew have devoted themselves to professional pleasantness. The care of passengers is often accompanied by permanent smiles and stylised loudspeaker voices. But among all this is the allure of the fashionable.

People-watching

So we start our descent. The cabin crew go around and collect the lists that we have obediently filled in. We are told where we will sit on the journey home and that our duty-free goods will be placed in plastic bags on our seats and that we may pay by credit card. Then a steep turn. There it is: we see first of all a volcano sticking up through the clouds and then we can look down towards Gran Canaria's large plastic greenhouses filled with tomatoes. Keenly we look up into the sky. Not a cloud in sight! The pilot tells us that it is plus twenty-four degrees on the ground. Wonderful!

As we taxi towards the flight terminal I notice through the cabin windows that the driver of the baggage lorry is wearing shorts. There is a breeze from the ocean. Across to the left are waving palm trees. We wait a quarter of an hour for our baggage and then off to the buses. Some passengers go straight out of the darkness of the airport terminal and sit eagerly on the baggage trolleys and warm their stiff bodies. Others wander around with their heavy cases looking for the right bus. Then the hire buses are on their way towards the town centre, *Playa des Ingles*. Longingly we look out through the bus windows. Bronzed tourists stroll along the hot asphalt roads. They have just come up from the beach. They have sun-bleached hair and squint as they observe our pale newly landed bodies. But soon even our hair will be ruffled. Sweden's grey winter is only five hours away.

So everything is repeated again: out onto the balcony, the obligatory appraisal of the view. Quickly off with winter clothes and on with a thinner shirt! Things quickly shoved into wardrobes and drawers! Where shall I hide my laptop – or shall I keep it with me all the time? A check for the closest *supermercado*, and off I go!

My pale skin is chapped after being indoors all winter. I listen to the sound of the sea breeze in the palms. I enter the water. After several hours I am sitting on a bench down by the sea while the moon comes up. Around me is a severely exploited coast. Every metre has been built on. With the best will in the world no-one could call this place beautiful. No, it is a place for relaxation, laziness and the smell of sun tan oil.

I spend several afternoons sitting on the long beach promenade – where people constantly pass by looking out to sea – and watch the passers-by. I am not alone. Like caged birds people sit in groups on the benches. The palm trees sway in the background. The bougainvillea spills over the chalk-white houses.

There is nothing quite as fascinating as watching other people. This can be noticed in all cultures – in cafés, in town squares and on street corners. The world's oldest, cheapest and most frequent enjoyment should be just that: 'people watching'. Perhaps it explains the attraction in sitting outside in the cool breeze while the afternoon sunshine is still strong and sipping a beer or a cappuccino.

Researchers are said to have found that the places that are most suitable for this pastime are those where one can watch others whilst remaining unobserved oneself. It seems that many people like to watch others 'from above, perhaps a left over from the era when people lived in trees'. Those places in cafés, parks or restaurants where the guests sit slightly raised, as if on shelves – where one has a good view without at the same time being too exposed – are always the first to be filled. Many people like to sit in the corner so that they are protected from the back.

Wide-eyed I read that psychologists tell us that this habit of sitting in dark corners and looking out over other people is a remainder of an evolutionary condition. Subconsciously people place themselves at the far back in a bar or up on a café stool to be able quickly to identify a potential enemy. This reptilian brain function has now been repressed, but the behaviour remains.

But to watch people *oneself* is only one side of the coin. It is also a question of displaying oneself. The café becomes an arena for a more testing social game. The Mediterranean beach promenades, but even more so the city boulevard cafés, are just the places for such a mixture of exhibitionism and voyeurism but it takes place in ordered and culturally established forms. Many people dress up and strut their stuff, both to see other people and to be admired themselves. It is just like that along the long beach promenade in San Augustin.

On the difficulty of taking time off

One morning I notice one of the other passengers from the plane – his wife is lying on a sunbed and reading a newspaper. He is sitting with a bottle of factor fifteen suncream in his right hand, in the other hand he has a mobile phone. During the course of the morning he goes over into the shade ten times to read his emails on the minute display. Apparently work has invaded his leisure time. I can hear him discussing business at the top of his voice, seemingly unperturbed, whilst pacing up and down in the park with his phone pressed to his ear. His wife looks at him from time to time and sighs.

For many people, holidays lead to disappointment: quite simply because they do not give themselves enough time to unwind. They discover that relaxing does not come automatically just because they are in a warm climate. They believe that they can go from a hundred percent activity to nothing. After having worked at full tempo up to the last minute, making long telephone calls and organizing all the practical arrangements, they dash on their way on a last-minute trip. On the plane they look through their diaries. But despite the fact that within a couple of hours they are standing in short-sleeved shirts, feeling the welcome sea breeze and the beer or white wine is cooling in the fridge, they still cannot relax. They rush down to some *supermercado*, return, flick through an evening paper and then sit and tap their fingers whilst the children jump up and down in the pool.

If someone is exhausted and burnt out they have difficulty in suddenly winding down and absorbing their surroundings in a more leisurely way. On the contrary, anything that takes time becomes unbearably irritating – they just cannot stand having to wait for anything or having to put up with nothing happening. Their brains are still functioning on overdrive.

Many people live with a daily information overload: telephones ringing; piles of bills to pay; children constantly demanding attention; post that never gets answered – everything is shouting: 'I am the most important! Deal with me first!' The brain registers this excessive amount of information by *directing its attention* to the most important facts and prioritizing them. But this very information system can be drained of its resources. People finally become irritated, exhausted and have difficulty making decisions. They become easily downcast and depressed. There are so many conflicting demands on their time. It is difficult to keep so many balls in the air at once. This is the situation for many travellers before they go away on holiday. No wonder that they are not capable of being happy or relaxed and that this induces a feeling of guilt.

Alongside this *directed attention* is a more *spontaneous* attention. This is more passive and accepting. This handles gentler stimuli which do not require any input. They need neither sorting, weighing nor evaluating. There is no need to make any decisions about them and they therefore do not need any energy expending on them – on the contrary they themselves give energy. These spontaneous stimuli are usually related to nature: a sea breeze, the rolling of the waves, the wind rustling the leaves on the trees, the twittering of birds and the feeling of the wind in one's hair. It takes a while for stressed people to loosen up and start to appreciate these small changes and nuances. The rediscovery of such gentle stimuli are thought to be especially beneficial for those who are 'burnt out' and in need of rehabilitation.

∽⊕∾

When I see the man in his newly pressed beige shorts rush off, yet again, to answer his telephone I think of the seventeenth-century philosopher Blaise Pascal's description of the centrifugal and centripetal movement. The workaholic has a way of distancing himself from his own being – he never starts the inner journey. He is finally so persecuted by external stimuli that the inward journey and the observation of gentler impressions never has a chance.

So what happens when someone has finally managed to let go and suddenly enters into a holiday mood of pleasurable indolence, and then against their will are forced into a state of directed attention again? They are intolerably irritated. A visit to a supermarket in the middle of a lazy holiday period can make their blood pressure rise. Several days of relaxing can be destroyed by a wait of several hours in a sticky queue. A telephone call from home just when one has finally managed to switch off can jangle the nerves for days. To open one's email every time one passes an Internet café or not switching off one's mobile can disrupt periods which ought to be important for relaxation.

The directed attention therefore can be a potential stress factor on any kind of trip. Sitting in traffic jams on roads on the autobahn or autostrada in Italy, or standing in a queue for tickets to get into some exhibition, squeezing through pedestrian streets in order to buy ice cream for the children or placating one's cultural conscience by looking at old ruins called monuments when it is as hot as hell, just as one had become used to lazily lying in the shade of a plane tree; such things are intolerable.

But the conscious lack of intention – which at the beginning is hard to overcome – is eventually transformed into the great relaxation. After several days many people notice the external world with its nuances: the flowers, insects, rustling leaves and the cypresses' majestic silhouette in the twilight. Nature is not just a backdrop to constant busyness – it is present, but its movements are still. Finally one realizes what the book is about and concentration returns.

What a view! What tranquillity!

One day I hire a scooter and ride inland. I am soon standing high up on the remains of an extinct volcano and looking down towards the blue Atlantic. Here there are signs carefully pointing out the most beautiful views. Even beauty is carefully packaged by the experience industry.

The worship of the beautiful parts of nature, wild or cultivated parks is an ancient idea. But the cult of the beautiful landscape is relatively recent. It began during the romantic period during the sixteenth and seventeenth centuries. People, especially from the bourgeoisie, went into raptures over mighty mountains, alpine pastures or ocean shores. The picturesque, anything that could be depicted in a painting, was important during the late seventeenth century. Down here in the Canary Islands hordes of people are standing along the beaches in the afternoon watching the weather-beaten fishermen come in with their catches.

Then, as now, people chose to travel to places they had already seen in paintings or heard about and which they in their turn could recount as memories. The evidence of this can be found in the postcard industry. This worship of the picturesque has spread across the entire world. In Europe this worship can mostly be seen among the Italian artists in the Piazza Navona in Rome where watercolours or oil paintings of walls covered in gaudy flowers are churned out as if on a conveyor belt. The self-proclaimed artists stand crushed together huddled near Montmartre in Paris producing the same view ten times a day under the admiring glances of blue-rinsed ladies from the USA – 'Isn't that cute?'

Most common of all are the black vendors who walk along the beaches selling African folk art.

The cult of silence also became distinct at the end of the nineteenth century. To wander respectfully near the buildings of antiquity meant that people could absorb the atmosphere of a bygone era. It created a link back to antiquity, to a rich and humanistic cultural inheritance. Even rambling through enchanting countryside became a source of relaxation for harassed city dwellers. The walking stick became a symbol of tranquillity. We can see the romanticism of the rambling nature lover in the writings of New England's transcendentalists such as Henry David Thoreau and Ralph Waldo Emerson. These memories can still be found in authors like John Cowper Powys, in the idealization of rambling, not to mention hearty German *Wandervögel* in central Europe. The Scout Association and the Tourist Association's marked trails in the Swedish country districts are remnants of this tradition.

Hikers in the Alps can still breathe fresh air whilst wandering along marked tracks. These are strictly regulated according to degree of difficulty and by obtaining special maps one can decide how long it will take to hike between two places in the Italian or French Alps. Some may even order a three-course dinner before they take a shower up in some *refugio* in the Italian mountains, especially if the climb has been steep. They can rest their legs whilst sitting in the evening twilight, looking out over the alpine scenery and feeling as if they are part of the cycle of nature. For many it is a spiritual experience.

But I am not hiking today. Instead I am zooming along the road on the hired streamlined scooter. No, the scenery cannot be called beautiful. The asphalt road is broken in places by long stretches of red-brown soil. The coastal view has been exploited. Rows of closely packed hotels are strung out along the coast. Partly-built hotels seem to outnumber those that are finished. Buses transport hot sticky groups of tourists along the roads. Building sites obscure the views and at every lay-by there are stalls selling bric-a-brac. The recurring visual enjoyment of this island is of course the food, the sun and the beach. However, the remains of the previous century's nature worship can be found in the newly built beach promenade which takes several hours to stroll along.

The man in the corner

It will soon be time to return to Sweden. By chance I am suddenly confronted with questions about another kind of journey, the inner journey. One day I go up to the mountains and creep into a little church. It is dark inside except for the light from a small votive light. Several elderly ladies are standing motionless gazing at an icon of the Virgin Mary. Then they bow and walk silently away after trimming the wicks of the candles. There is a confessional just inside the door. The kneeler is well worn and I look at the small grille between the priest and the penitent and think of all the sins that have been revealed through this partition of metal holes. But I stand mainly motionless and gaze at the icon hanging beside the altar. It is dirty and grimy with the smoke from decades of candles. But the eyes can be seen shining through the dirt.

While I am standing in the church another tourist enters. He has his shirt hanging out and is carrying a thick novel and a map. He also stands completely still for a while. Neither of us speaks. Outside the small chapel we can hear buses and cars. The other man squints against the light when we come out into the sun again, we nod in greeting and I go back to write.

Later that evening I turn off my computer, tired of the flickering of the screen and take myself down to the beach promenade. Music can be heard from some of the hotels. The sound from the sea is noticeable. I drop down onto a bench just as the man from the church walks past. We sit by the sea talking. He becomes animated when he hears that I am involved with religion. After a while we go our separate ways.

Later I see him sitting in a corner in one of the eating places down by the shore. We greet each other again and I sit down and join him. It is then that he says: 'I often go into churches. I think that they create a feeling of tranquillity. But I do not understand how anyone can believe in a deity.' We sit looking out over the Atlantic, red and gold oranges hanging up on the roof and the palm trees swaying. He continues, almost rudely: 'For me the actual church is enough, but it seems completely improbable to believe that there is some heavenly figure somewhere who actively engages in human life. There is no evidence for it. As far as I understand humans have been cast out into an empty and echoing universe. Of course, I realize well enough that *mankind* has always created gods for itself, spirits and guardians, Mary, Jesus and Buddhas and such like. Everyone needs some type of security figure to cling to – especially in a crisis. But to believe that there is some sort of deity *within* or *outside* this existence? No, forgive me for saying it, but I think that this is a classic case of wishful thinking.'

Several elderly ladies walk past carrying trays laden with cakes and coffee cups. Some people are sitting in faded bathing clothes in the warm evening, others are dressed up for the evening. Glowing from the day's hot sun they are waiting for their orders, several children are whining for more ice cream. The man in the corner lights another cigarette and looks at me without blinking. He continues: 'I can't get away from the feeling that all religions stem from self-delusion. Religion is interesting, beautiful and attractive. I love the tranquillity and beauty of churches. Furthermore I believe that many people are made happy by religion. But I find it hard to believe that there is something "out there" which fulfils their longing. You must remember Doctor Relling in Ibsen's *Wild Duck* who says, "If you take away a lifelong deception from a human being you take away happiness at the same time." And the talk of His famous goodness is often shown to be overestimated. Just think of 11 September 2001 or the events of 2003. On those particular days He seems to have been elsewhere. It is rather bad planning by someone who guarantees benevolence, one

could say. Of course I understand that mankind is weak.
But despite the popularity of religious fantasies and the way
that they work – in that people have gained solace from
them for millennia – doesn't necessarily mean that they are
true, does it? And what about us? We don't lie awake at
night worrying about lack of meaning but we come here to
sunbathe and enjoy ourselves, what would they do with us?'

We have a marathon discussion about life's journey and
uncertainty about faith, about outward and inner journeys,
on evil, love and God. But we also discuss the black doubts
about futility, the feelings of claustrophobia and how no-
one can flee from themselves. Then we go our separate
ways.

The icon in my pocket

Standing in the middle of the crowds streaming up and
down from the shopping centre in San Augustin is a tipsy
man with red cheeks and a loud voice. He has a strong beer
in one hand and a plastic bag with bathing clothes and a
large bag in the other. He is singing the old revivalist song:
'Over there the morning is dawning, and at home the saints
are assembling.' Perhaps he is right, I think to myself as I
walk towards my hotel. Who knows? Who can say?

When I get back to the hotel I take out the small icon
which I often carry in my pocket. It is from Russia and only
measures a few square centimetres. It was given to me
several years ago by some children in Murmansk. It is
plastic and is made in the form of a triptych. It looks like a
miniature altar screen. It is an iconostasis which can be
folded up in an ingenious way. On the left sits the Virgin
Mary with the child Jesus, the middle icon is of Christ
Pantocrator – Ruler of all – and on the right is St Nicholas
looking at me with a steady, serious gaze. When it is folded
it is as small as a credit card. It is my travel icon. No, I don't
keep it in my wallet. That would be irreverent. I usually
carry it in my jacket or trouser pocket along with pencil
stubs, loose change and some fluff. Sometimes I place it

open on my desk, a café table or at the side of the bed.

A barely noticeable, but seriously calm gaze looks back at me from the cheap Russian plastic. The reverse perspective of the icon means that the observer is always observed wherever he is. Or rather – the observer is drawn into the icon's world. The muted colours of the minute pictures, dark red, gold and light blue, light up my office. The icon watches over me while I sleep on train journeys or drowse at airports. It is placed next to my bed when I come home. At present it is placed on the railing of a balcony several miles off the coast of Africa. But usually it sits in my pocket. Holiness doubly concealed.

I look at the little icon with its inscrutable eyes whilst I ponder over the 'man in the corner'. His questioning is also mine. Is the observer in actual fact merely gazing into his own projected wishful thinking? Is there anything hidden there – in the eyes of the icon – something else, simply an Other? I believe it, but who knows? Only God can be his own guarantor.

But I place the icon back in my pocket and begin my packing. I clean the little kitchen. I sit for a while on the balcony watching the sunset and glancing at the computer, every now and then moving a word or two around. The hours pass. Soon there will only be one night left in this mild part of the world. Tomorrow it will be the same procedure again: bus, the airport's elegant boredom, the tax-free shops, the crowds and the smell of perfume. In only twelve hours I will be sitting on the train to Uppsala – I heard today that it is minus six degrees and dull up there. But at the moment it is still warm. I remain sitting and listen to the ocean sighing like a slow exhalation of breath.

Chapter Two

THE FASCINATION AND MELANCHOLY OF TRAVEL

Tourist, backpacker and vagabond

Back home again I return to the question: What are we travelling *towards* and what are we getting away *from*? I look through some research about tourism. As we have seen, there are many different words for travellers. These can be listed according to a hierarchy, but they are all simplified stereotypes. Right at the bottom of the scale comes the word *tourist*. Most people seem to regard this word as slightly negative and want to distance themselves from the image that it conjures up. Perhaps they are thinking about Stig Helmer's hairstyle in the 1980s film, *Package Tour,* or Hawaiian shirts and long drinks at Peppe and Anita's bar in Las Palomas. (Which incidentally is still there. I've seen it.)

Despite the fact that most travellers go on package tours, they do not like to admit it. To be shepherded round in groups, to sit in warm, cramped buses or to walk in line with yellow baseball caps on, is not something that most people will admit to. Then the talk of being a solitary *flâneur* or vagabond seems more attractive – not least for intellectuals or young people. Round these words there clings an aura of urbanity which rubs off on the person saying them.

The global backpacker culture is an industry in itself with only a few decades of history but with a wealth of glossy magazines. The aim is to create expectations and myths about *the unique* in both the traveller and the destination:

create your own ultimate journey! Travel magazines show pictures of the adventure travellers' sun-bleached hair. There are endless tales of the solitary long distance traveller who is away for six months. Many of them want to make a film or write a book about their travels. To dive in far off oceans, meditate with monks in India or moonlight in Harlem or Cuba is as attractive for young people on the verge of adulthood, as white sands are heavenly for exhausted families with children, who can leave their offspring in the children's pool – well covered in sunscreen factor eighteen.

The cultural traveller is considered – at least in their own eyes – to have a higher status, and to belong to the travelling elite. They claim not to understand the charms of camping. Those who do not travel to small towns in Liguria but go to densely packed beaches instead or who prefer Burger King to Italian cuisine are looked on with mild disdain. For culture vultures in search of tranquillity and a deepening of historical experience, the hordes of noisy groups with a skinful of beer and a spring in their steps are pushy and vulgar. This can lead to a clash. Those who have the poet Dante in their minds and the artist Titian in their travel guides are forced into unwanted and close proximity with tourists who, when in an Italian trattoria, would rather have a large beer and watch League football.

But all these simplistic stereotypes – the charter tourists, backpackers, *flâneur* – are in their turn about to be crushed. Individual travel behaviour is changing. The post or late modern person seems in actual fact to go on *both* charter holidays, cultural holidays *and* adventure holidays. Travel patterns change over time and during the same person's life cycle. Travel agencies arrange tailor-made holidays which will suit the twenty-first century individual. To sail round the Greek Islands can be just as attractive for them as a week in a guest house in Tromsö on their next holiday when they can sleep away a week. The same individual can one year hike in the Jämtland mountains and the next season purchase a cruise between the Bahamas and Key West, dive off the Barrier Reef or sunbathe in Tenerife. Travel styles seem to be more and more fractured.

Stereotypes, such as the package tourist's alleged superficiality and the cultural tourist's renowned depths seem to be relatively permanent. But according to one researcher who has interviewed travellers in a typical tourist destination in Portugal, several different styles of tourist seem to exist.

The aim of the recreational tourists is to get away. They want to spend a lot of time together. They are content with a couple of outings but prefer the sun lounger by the pool. They want to have a cosy time, preferably with their nearest and dearest or someone they have met on a bus tour or on the beach. They keep away from noisy discos and crowded bars. They want to have a restful time and are happy not to have to worry about any of the practicalities.

The same researcher found that another group, the cultural tourists, wanted to do something educational the whole time. 'We haven't come here just to lie still and perspire!' They look for museums to visit as well as exhibitions, gardens and concerts. But at the same time they keep to themselves. Many of them make sure that they are well prepared before their trip. They have often 'read up' about the places and often have a checklist with them from home of all the things that they want to see in the time: they carry maps and guide books. Despite the fact that they have travelled by charter they like to pretend that they are not tourists. They are used to considering themselves as special.

Adventure tourists are often younger. They also want something to be happening the whole time, but they prefer something more exciting and want to be with other like-minded people. The go on diving courses, hire water scooters, surf and look for excitement and entertainment. They are tempted by the bars and late nights. But at the same time the restlessness is obvious. A boring and uneventful holiday is the worse thing that can happen to them.

Gap Year travel

For many young people, the planning, carrying out, documenting and talking about Gap Year travel (preferably alone, long and full of hardship), has been one of the rich countries' most important rites of passage. At one time it was Confirmation that defined someone as an adult, then the A level exams fulfilled the same function. But now it seems that it is not until they have made their first long trip that young people are classed as adults. In these circles anyone who *hasn't* travelled is considered unusual, practically exotic: 'What! Have you never been abroad? What are you saying? Don't you *want* to travel?'

By spending months – sometimes years – on their travels in several continents, the gap widens between childhood's routine school existence and the adult world's approaching demands: childbearing, work and the dreaded 'Mr Average' existence. By planning, travelling – and then remembering their travels – they become visible and avoid being absorbed into the vague landscape of 'Mr/Ms Average'. The wind of travel means that existence is tangible, it can be *felt*. They are probably completely oblivious to the fact that their own entry into adulthood is slowly taking place.

It is unthinkable to many backpackers to use charter flights. For them the most important thing is unplanned adventure trips, high risk travel and trips to challenging places. One travel guide is called *Dangerous Places*. Others offer advice on macabre travel destinations. It seems that it is no longer the place that is the most important but that the travellers can maximize their *experiences*. The focus is neither on nature, history nor culture; but rather on physical experiences. The traveller wants to feel that he exists.

Travel has of course always been a part of becoming adult and mature: to break away, to flex one's wings alone and then to come home and tell people about it. But the interest in extreme sports and the fascination of dangerous places is perhaps a more or less desperate attempt to escape from the western world's cushioned and constricted nanny state.

What is now happening in the first years of the twenty-first century is that more and more older people are following the young people's travel patterns. Not even here can the children of the seventies be left in peace. The children of the forties are invading their global space.

But soon even the globetrotting backpacker generation will be in their forties. Finally they will not be able to joke about gathering 'adult points' without sounding pathetic. Neither will they be able to put off making serious decisions about their lives by going off on yet more journeys. After several years, the backpack is exchanged for children's clothes, teddy bears and toys packed in colourful bags. Those people who several years earlier partied the night away on the beaches of the southern hemisphere are now leaning back and watching their kids in the children's pool in the Canaries or on Crete whilst reading the tabloid newspapers from home. When the children are asleep they sit on their balconies listening to the thud of the disco in the distance.

Gap Year travel has become a kind of identity marker. Many can remember the exact year that they travelled, where to and with whom. In the necklace of years that they look back on, the long trip shines like a diamond. Often these memories are connected to places one has visited. It is often trivial memories such as 'That was the time that I burnt my back the first day and you fell off a camel' or 'It was when you stood in a swimming pool and taught the kids to dive' or 'It was when we were sitting outside in the evening. I'll never forget when the birds started singing at four-thirty in the morning just as it was getting light.'

A centrifugal culture

Now let us switch perspective and think socially rather than geographically by looking at travel as a metaphor or a picture of mankind's place in society.

A person who once upon a time saw himself as a pilgrim – with a set goal, ideologically, religiously or politically –

has now begun to be replaced by another type of person; the unattached drifter. For many post-modern people the hunt for new experiences seems to be more important than the ultimate goal, strategic thinking and planning. The present seems to be more important than the future, the individual more important than the group, authenticity more important than flexibility, and independence more valuable than community spirit. Excitement and maximization of experiences have been placed in the centre of life. The focus is rarely geared towards collective solidarity, patriotism, changing society or furthering a political or religious ideal. What many people want to 'find' is themselves.

This experience-orientated individualization arises at the same time as interest in party politics is waning. The well-thought-out ideologue takes even less with him on his 'charter travel' towards a common goal: the socialist, liberal or Marxist society. This does not mean that religion, questions of life or politics should be considered unimportant – on the contrary. But large institutions and ever ready answers are mistrusted. Collective Utopias seem to have withered away despite the fact that there are strong opposing forces against them in organizations such as Attac, (Advanced Tradewars Tactical Assault and Combat), the environmental movement *Reclaim the City* or the Swedish mission to the cities project. The idealogues' 'charter tourists' are becoming fewer whilst the political 'vagabonds' are increasing. There are fewer 'party faithful' than ever and churches, trades unions, Temperance and ideological movements are losing members. A lot revolves around the individual with the constantly repeated mantra 'You make your own luck!' The demand for maximization of experiences and the emphasis on instant gratification are obvious.

This wandering egocentric lifestyle and the aimless confusion can certainly be interpreted in socio-political or economic terms. But the restless gaze and the hunt for The Great Adventure can also be interpreted as an expression of a fundamental existential homelessness – *an anxiety of heart.* The search for 'something more' can be seen as an expression of a lack of meaning – perhaps quite simply a kind of metaphysical anaemia. Many people seem dissatisfied. They are afflicted by emptiness if they have to stop rushing hither and thither in a disharmonious culture. Perhaps they dare not slow down otherwise they would start asking themselves anxious questions. 'I don't know where I'm going, therefore it is important to get a move on!' Perhaps the *wanderlust* is a way of treading water on top of a feeling of melancholy and inner desolation?

Most people in the secular West mistrust the thought that life should have a centre. The much praised postmodernity demands instead that existence is decentralized. Since all values are temporary there is neither centre nor periphery. Most of them are social constructions. It is no wonder that relativism creates vertigo and that people look around for alternatives.

The centrifugal forces in the culture which Pascal talked about are tangible. Through an excess of alternatives, information forced on us by the Internet, the enforced intimacy of the telephone and its self-proclaimed right constantly to disturb people, the difficulty of defending oneself against the terrors of advertising and consumerism, the opportunities for relaxation and reflection become commodities in short supply. Silence becomes a luxury. Thanks to the constant demand for attention, quick meetings and passing contacts the feeling that other people are present in our lives finally lessens. In a centrifugal culture more and more people are becoming alienated from a simple and obvious identity, a stable feeling of who one is. People are constantly being wrenched up to the surface of their own personalities. Therefore the opposing, the centripetal forces – the inner journeys are becoming more important.

Put into sociologists' terms: when most things have become splintered and none of the social norms give stability, more and more things seems to revolve around *the ego*. But at the same time there is no peace or obvious identity; this must constantly be reclaimed. Through all this the

advertising campaigns and the mass media exert their forcefully exploitative powers. They invest enormous sums of
money and then sit back to wait for success by increasing
people's insecurities so that they then can offer goods and
services that they claim will alleviate this artificially induced
dissatisfaction. If we read through a typical magazine we
soon notice that we are being urged to *replace* everything.

The house must be refurbished; the body must be
slimmer, the hair darker, the skin more glowing and the car
larger. If we were to say that the house should remain
unchanged or let the body's ageing process take its course
or quite simply say that we are happy as we are, we would
be considered suspect or immoral. As *homo consumens* –
Man the Consumer – we are invited to purchase ourselves
an acceptable self-image. By buying designer clothes, furniture and sports gear people state who they are. One of these
lifestyle products is the successful holiday: 'This is the ultimate holiday destination; here you will live life, *real*
genuine life. This is a *unique* holiday, it is tailor made just
for *you*.' There is a hidden message here. Everyday life
involving work, nursery, homework and a few hours sunk
in front of the TV is trivialized and slightly shameful.

But there is a contrasting picture. The need for an ideological and spiritual re-centering is on the way back.
Pilgrimages are slowly starting to be valued again. Visits to
monasteries and retreat house have undergone a renaissance. People go on pilgrimages to newly discovered old
destinations, interest in history is increasing, and books on
new spirituality are selling even more than before. But in
the consumer culture the opposite is usually the case, the
flâneur is idealized. The nomad – the one who only occa-
sionally puts down roots – is thought by many to be a more
attractive option than the farmer who calmly sows his fields
or the pilgrim who strives towards a specific goal. The latter
are sometimes considered as romantic idealists, remainders
of a disillusioned group of survivors from 1968. But a new
generation is now discovering the inner journey via the
outward.

The classical pilgrimage destinations were previously Nidaros Cathedral in Trondheim, Santiago de Compostela in Spain, St Peter's Basilica in Rome, the Temple in Jerusalem or – for Muslims – the Kaba in Mecca. Religious pilgrimages were a mixture of inner and outward journeys. The pilgrim was convinced that there really was a centre to existence – an original home – and that one could meet this centre in a specific geographical location. That is why they travelled there. Perhaps it is this need to re-centre that we are witnessing when we read about the increased interest in pilgrimages.

Let us now combine the reasoning behind the outward and inner journey. One way of interpreting the continually roving lifestyle is that it offers a refuge from the things that people feel that they are going to meet: inner desolation. Anything arising from within does not stand a chance if someone is constantly in motion. But it is also possible to reverse the perspective. During a journey an individual can get nearer to themselves, reach their own centre or quite simply the centre of existence. The geographical journey's inner movement goes in two opposite directions; it can be a way of *fleeing from* oneself. But it can also offer an opportunity *to catch up with* oneself.

Mint tea in Algiers

A solitary Scandinavian tourist is sitting with an empty glass of mint tea at a rickety table in the corner of a square in a North African coastal town. The rest of the tour group have gone to bed. A grey-black night. Crickets in the background, fireflies flash in the cool darkness. First she is meditating over the people walking past, a restful pursuit – the oldest in the world. But after a while her gaze stops observing the outside world. Her attention turns inward. She draws a little with a biro on a serviette as she is transported back in time. She is trying to determine her position. She is looking into the corners of her memory and wondering why her life turned out as it did.

Later in the hotel she closes the window onto the pool. But she still can't sleep, despite the fact that she is finally on holiday and that the velvet night is mild, that the dinner was good, the children have run around in their sun hats on the beach and the other members of the group are good company. In the middle of the holiday that she has looked forward to for months and has finally been able to achieve, she starts on another type of journey. As long as everything is as usual she never manages to catch up with herself – or rather her inner being never manages to catch up with her. But no; old rubbish forms a vault, plans that have come to nothing, sorrows that will never be healed and then this vague feeling that everything has passed so quickly. Of course, there is also the pleasure in the new food and spices, good books, long conversations, the children's laughter, her husband's tenderness. She is fascinated by the chirp of the crickets and the moon which in the southern hemisphere seems to hang at the wrong angle. She stands for a while on the balcony watching the palms swaying.

We observe some other travellers. A tired twenty-six-year-old seasonal visitor who has windsurfed the whole day and now sits slumped in front of a computer in the Internet café in Fuerteventura. He has read his emails. So he stares into space. He stares for several minutes out to sea. His gaze is turned both inwards and outwards. On Rhodes a man sits who has been swimming with his friends. Now he has slipped away to get some peace. He is sitting quietly on a balcony drinking beer and smoking. He stares out towards the black booming waves. A middle-aged man in the Caffè Florian in Venice feels a melancholy feeling come creeping over him. Tired of himself he puts down a novel by Franz Kafka and looks out over the bobbing gondolas. His gaze is also directed inwards.

Somewhere in *The history of silence and other essays,* Peter Englund discusses the Norwegian philosopher, Lars Svendsen. 'The paradox in melancholy is therefore that in its complete feeling of meaninglessness it in fact does have a meaning.' It has a meaning 'because man is bored because life lacks a goal and meaning and the task is to make us aware of exactly that', it is a 'source of insight ... the lack of meaning ... connects melancholy to modernity and its breakthrough. Modern technology as you know creates a lack of meaning if it "increasingly makes us into passive observers and consumers, and to a lesser degree, active participants" at the same time that secularization and lack of history also cuts us off from the meaning which has come to us since time immemorial in the form of religion or tradition.'

The melancholy of life's journey

Sometimes an outward journey activates suppressed thoughts about the passage of time, that man is just a traveller. He is carried slowly through his life's journey, from the trusting and simple world of childhood, through the enthusiasm of youth, the uncertainty about decisions that must be taken from the multitude of alternatives that are on offer, the expansive period of adulthood, the drudgery and happiness of middle age, to the insidious nagging insight of old age, that wonderful things are transitory. In everyday life this rootlessness can be hidden, laughed away or buried in hectic activity. But then he falls into a culture-free zone, on a beach or by a pool. When he has seen enough of pyramids, snorkelled in warm seas or gazed in wonderment at Thai temples, other thoughts come to the fore. Finally he can no longer run from himself.

But also when we look at the reminders of travel: the photo albums or dusty souvenirs – artefacts from this life – we look directly into the journey of life. We think to ourselves: 'What wonderful times we had' or 'The children were so small then'. thankfulness for everything that we have been part of is combined with something else. We do not look forward with such simple and genuine happiness, but often calculate how long we have left – something that was unthinkable only a few years ago.

Perhaps it is just a reaction against the realization that

this journey through life will end, which makes the complete opposite – the summer cottage- something which *must* remain unchanged. The same comics and magazines from the sixties and seventies must remain in the window frames. Granny's straw hat must be on the hall shelf. Time must stand still in the summer cottage – adolescent children are often the most conservative, nothing in the cottage must be changed! However, even in the peace of the cottage, in the familiar old garden, on the beach by the sea, along the paths through the wood – places where everything remains the same – we can see in relief how our own journey through time continually progresses. We are mirrored in the unchanging. Unnoticed we are all transported along the limited length of life's axis.

But what happens if a person actively attempts to avoid rushing through life and deliberately puts the brakes on? In the anonymity of a journey when everyday conventions cease, we become aware of a wonderment that we would not otherwise have noticed. On the treadmill of everyday life and family concerns, few have time to ponder over the big questions. What is our life for, how will we bear the thought that our life must come to an end, if there is an overall purpose to life, if God exists or if everything is just the work of chance?

People about to make important decisions, those who have gone through a divorce or who are grieving for a loved one often take themselves off on a package holiday or visit a city just to find time to get an overview. They may travel alone with just their diary for company or they may go with a friend. The journey creates a pause for reflection and sets a parenthesis round everyday life. Then the inner journey is planned. Others relate that they have been affected by an incomprehensible sadness when the children finally leave home and working life has lost its sheen. They realize with a pang that they have less time left of their life's journey than that which has gone before. In such cases the inner journey is spontaneous.

The inner journey has no glossy catalogues. There are no

last-minute offers. It is a lot more diffuse, but precisely because of this it is neglected. It is as much about life's intensity as a halt caused by an indeterminate anxiety. The departure takes place when someone has looked through hearty tips on how to be happy, and has had enough of philosophical and cultural deep thinking: when the need for a greater seriousness is unavoidable.

But to avoid any misconceptions: of course most of us travel out into the world because it is exciting, renewing, culturally enriching, relaxing, and fun, restful, sunny, and instructive. Most of the time we don't think for a second about the meaning of life and it is just as well. We are busy enjoying the food and the company of our friends, sun and laughter, culture and history. But there is a hidden zone beyond the stereotypes of travel.

The pilgrim – a disappearing species?

We have seen that there were once a great many travellers making pilgrimages. Hither and thither they travelled to be close to holiness. They travelled to holy springs, to places where there had been miracles or an apparition. Their main reason for travelling was neither relaxation, culture nor enlightenment. No, here existential anxiety could be linked to a place which gave meaning and stability to existence. These pilgrims seek out places that are endowed with a spiritual strength – places which represent the centre of existence. When they reach their goal they linger for a long time in front of an icon. Others make for monasteries in the Egyptian deserts or the mountains of the Himalayas. Why? Perhaps because only a pilgrimage is connected to a completely different side of life than consumption, enjoyment and culture: the need for a centre.

From a scientifically religious perspective one can – along with all economic, social and political reasons for the perpetual motion of the modern day – add the feeling of rootlessness which arises when the lack of belonging becomes tangible. *When one doesn't know where one is going it is tempting to increase speed.* Route maps, political as well as religious, are changing all the more rapidly. Each person must therefore create their own overview and try to tread as best they can.

Perhaps the chase after great experiences – not least on holiday – is a replacement for the loss of steering, an attempt to make the compass stop spinning. It seems sometimes that it is only when someone has been part of something exceptional or different that it is completely real: 'I feel, therefore I exist.' 'How does it feel?' seems to be the new millennium's perhaps most frequently asked question. Perhaps it is more usual than: 'What do you think?' The pendulum has swung from opinions to feelings.

Perhaps that is why the journey and the retelling of it has become such a central part of a person's identity building. People show who they are by relating which countries they have visited or plan to visit. They state their position by stating which places they absolutely would *not* visit. It is as if the person comes into existence in the actual movement of travel. To remain motionless would be the same as annihilation. Against this the Latin maxim remains crystal clear – *hic locus sanctus est* – this is the holy place. It is not possible to flee from oneself.

Chapter Three

COLLECTING EXPERIENCES

The packaged experience

We have all seen him. The elderly Greek priest with the lined face and long beard who sits on an ancient wooden chair against a bleached white wall, calmly smoking a cigarette. In the background an azure blue sea. Down below are several fisherman drawing in their nets. On the table stands a glass of ouzo or retsina. That was the stereotypical travel poster twenty or thirty years ago. Nowadays it is more likely to be Aztec temples, Vietnamese war cemeteries or Greenland icebergs.

I flick, more or less systematically, through piles of travel magazines and attempt to understand. Most are about the charms of travel, the hunt for something original but at the same time the pictures exude a sense of urgent haste, the need to see as much as possible and to document everything. Soon it will have disappeared. But 'we have the genuine article!'

Mostly one is offered prefabricated and packaged experiences. The tourist industry produces actual goods such as plastic chairs, drinks or hotel beds. It even sells services such as baby sitting, cleaning, breakfast in the room, pig roasts or diving courses. But above all it produces experiences for the senses and 'discoveries'. Tour guides offer controlled euphoria and stage managed spontaneity: rambling, diving, climbing or white-water rafting – all for large sums of money.

The experience industry has fallen into the claws of global capitalism. Standardization becomes all the more tangible. 'Genuine' experiences are constructed by advertisements, packaged by guide books or TV programmes and consumed by the western world's young people or pensioners who glide around the world with their mobiles with in-built cameras in one hand and a Visa card in the other.

What started out as 'getting away from it all', often as a kind of anti-consumerism, has gradually been transformed into large companies which *package* everything; from views, transport systems, snacks, spiritual experiences and souvenirs – with the object of being consumers. Because of this a great many employment opportunities are created. 'Pre-programming' of how successful the trip will be is impossible to get away from. It has been created by generations of travellers, by the travel industry's marketing and the recommendations of friends. Travel experiences fall between the deeply personal – those which we experience privately – and those which are predetermined by the expectations created by the advertisements. The myth of the new experience is in itself a construction.

The most practical way of achieving the truly exotic should therefore be to get hold of one of the commonest travel handbooks – preferably the *Lonely Planet* guide – and a good map and then systematically seek out those places which are *not* mentioned. There will perhaps soon be a more important travel trend – to travel in the opposite direction, to visit towns which start with the letter L or the collect postcards of unusual bridges or to climb church towers in India or to read a half-forgotten historical biography and then travel in the subject's footsteps.

Collecting journeys instead of things

In a culture that has accustomed itself to material things circulating at an ever-increasing speed – anything that is permanent evaporates – the collection of journeys becomes of vital importance. When things erode – the interest in

consumer items is on its way out in the over-commercial-
ized West, they are made obsolete within the course of days
or even hours, people demand 'experiences' instead. By
filling their lives with things that are not material, vivid
memories, rather than by purchasing new furniture or other
consumer items they increase their chances of being part of
something 'unique': 'That was a real experience!'

Perhaps a great deal of travel can be interpreted as a kind
of anti-culture. The circulation of commercially mass-
produced products, clothes and globally anonymous
designer labels means that anything individual is fast disappearing In an increasingly standardized society opposite
trends are emerging. Perhaps that is why it has become so
important to collect something (apparently) unique. The
faster that the significance of external things diminishes, the
greater is the need of experiences which (in an idealized
form) remain in the individual's memory. Psychologizing
has replaced materializing. By seeking out that something
special a person can show their originality and avoid disappearing into the hated grey masses. The journey itself is part
of the project of 'being somebody special', being an individual. 'When my life has run its course at least I will be
able to say that I have had experiences , I have really lived.'

Find Paradise on earth!

Within the word 'travel' itself there often lies a romanticiz-
ing of anything different, anything that is not 'as usual'. But
the idealization of the different contributes to a trivializing
of the everyday: 'This old town with its shopping centres,
shoe shops and shuffling pensioners with their rollators in
the pedestrian streets – can that be worth anything?' We
tend to think when we see bronzed bodies on TV who are
either wading through the wet grass of a jungle, grappling
with crocodiles or watching antelope spring across the path
'At home the most we can expect to see are a few rabbits or
deer glimpsed at the side of the road.' The undervalued
charms of the everyday are hidden under the media's images

of the Good Life. That is to be found somewhere else. There is an enormous economic potential in the travel industry's method of emphasizing the image of the boring everyday by overemphasizing the appeal of the exotic.

The idea, or rather the myth, of the original paradise exists as an important concept in the whole of the West's cultural history. In some of the travel advertisements casual offers arise for the 'pure healthy life'. This could be a South Sea island with guaranteed 'genuine' primitive inhabitants, a cowboy ranch where one can still ride bareback or Lapps who 'yoik' around open fires in Jokkmokk. In the longing for the primitive an evolutionary concept of time is hidden. If it states in the guide books that tourists are offered tea/ fishing/ hunting seal with the 'local inhabitants who have lived here for a thousand years', these visitors feel that they can escape from the stresses of civilization for a few days. It is as if there were a 'true reality' underneath the boring veneer of culture.

Nostalgia for the past is often combined with both a kind of primitivism and a veiled criticism of culture: It is necessary to visit these remnants of ancient civilizations before it is too late. Backpackers especially are engaged in a race against time. They must reach the 'genuine' before it has been destroyed, economically exploited or spoilt by the all-too-frequent presence of other tourists.

But even the search for the genuine can be commercialized. Day trips to the sacred dances in village temples turn out to be bus tours to a temple full of collapsible plastic chairs, rickety tables and Sprite cans. After the performance the dancers shrug off their beautiful folk costumes and put on their T-shirts with 'Hard Rock Cafe' on. They make calls on their mobiles and take off into the night on their mopeds.

And I think that the idea of 'the unique' must clearly be a bait for the entire tourist industry. When the talk of something genuine is spread to ever-larger groups of travellers it becomes paradoxically even more difficult to achieve. Yesterday's untouched travel goal will all too soon become tomorrow's tourist trap.

Cultural dilution and mental claustrophobia

Life's increasing standardization is becoming more and more tangible both nationally and globally. If you look carefully at town centres and squares in Swedish towns you can see the same half-empty roadside restaurants with blond interiors and stewed coffee in Falun, Halmstad or Skellefteå. In northern Europe you can find the same gleaming metal caffe latte bars in all the cities. These are where the beautiful people hang out. The bleached department store furnishings are confusingly alike. The same clothes chains have similar window displays in Uppsala, Krakow or Barcelona.

The cappuccino machines hiss out their cultural message over the entire world. Designer clothes logos block out the individual ethnic and national lines. The same exotic food dishes are served in restaurants in Kiruna, Laholm or London. At one time pizza was unusual in northern Europe. Now there is Chinese food, spicy Thai and Vietnamese cuisine virtually everywhere. Cultural and geographical characteristics are gradually sinking without trace. American baseball caps are perched on the heads of rickshaw drivers in Cambodia. Orthodox priests in Egypt talk into their Nokia telephones and the Thai chef in St Petersburg regularly checks his email. Whatever has happened to the exotic?

You can travel for a long way without reaching anything foreign or unfamiliar; far away appears to be getting closer. You move forward without reaching your destination. Wherever you set out for you are always at home. The Welfare Society's global network of standardized advertisers and brand names creates a mental inertia.

In all this one can sense a latent panic at being imprisoned on this little globe. The internet, tour operator price wars and even cheaper telephone charges means that the grand leave-taking, and the constant hope that a loved one will get in touch, have disappeared. Words such as longing, preparation and nostalgia seem to be slowly disappearing.

Now the important thing is *direct access*. *On line* is more important than *on time*. Whatever happened to longing?

Wherever you are in the world you are soon on familiar ground; every square centimetre of the globe has been mapped and *www* blinks out just the same at home, when staying with friends or at an airport in Laos or Berlin. Everything is accessible everywhere – at the same time. GPS (Global Positioning System) reaches the whole world. The world has become easier to cope with like a giant village. At the same time it has taken on a more clearly claustrophobic atmosphere. Where can you travel to if the whole world is devastatingly the same?

At a time when the world is threatened by global warming and an unequal economic distribution that is catastrophic, Africans are standing with hungry eyes staring into Europe's well-stocked gardens. When people look out over the heated towns and think about last year's catastrophic floods, under the thin ozone layer the sun feels like a blowtorch. There is a documentary film that shows the earth from a satellite. In ninety minutes you can make one circuit around this glistening pearl in the blackness of the universe. The clear knowledge that this globe is gliding through the cosmos like Harry Martinson's space ship *Aniara,* means that many people feel as if they are a speck of dust in the emptiness of the universe. It is therefore not surprising that there are threatening instincts which man will avoid at all costs. Arranging new experiences is one way of escaping from the inner weariness, but is it simply a means of avoiding the journey into one's own inner being?

How many people say in the middle of a trip 'It feels as if I am in a film.' If you drink a quiet beer on a cliff top in the Swedish archipelago it feels as if you are part of a Pripps beer advertisement. When someone arrives in Manhattan, New York, for the first time in his life he almost expects to meet the main characters in the film *Crocodile Dundee* or if he lands in Los Angeles perhaps a *Beverley Hills Cop* will pass by. Reference points are all too often taken from the world of the media. As if this fantasy world were the true one.

The constant comparing of experiences says something about the present need to be deeply moved by something and not to let life trickle away in a meaningless procession of days. But the demand for great experiences finally leads to cultural wear and tear. After far too high expectations, and long hours sitting and waiting at stressful airports, all that is left is a feeling of weariness and emptiness: 'I hardly dare admit it, but all I want to do is to go home!'

Capturing reality on film – on being 'snap-happy'

In nearly every travel bag there is a camera packed with the sun lotion, beach towel, telephone and cigarettes. Several times on holiday I may take pictures of people standing in front of a view, a restaurant, a white cruise ship in a harbour. Why so many photographs? If you were to ask someone what was the most important thing they have in their homes many of them would answer their photograph albums. Perhaps this is because pictures help us to form a structure of our own lives – they create a lifeline where we remember what we have done and when. By looking at the album's yellowing pages constructed out of our own journeys through life, we can point out the stopping places. The pictures are a way of conserving time.

The photo album can be seen as a thread running through the story of our lives. To sort through piles of printed pictures or look through the photos saved in our computers, and then stick them into albums is one of the few occasions when modern city folk can be creative. By keeping a diary of their travels, putting pictures in a folder, drawing sketches and maps, gluing in concert tickets and receipts for once we are in control of our own lives.

Some make jokes about this constant photography. Mr Typical Tourist is often a stiff Japanese who stands as straight as a rod on a photo in front of a grey monument in one of the world's cities. Some people seem so occupied with recording their travels that they don't seem to be able to live except via their objective. They become anxious if they have not taken enough photos or they can fret for decades over lost reels of film or erased pictures. It seems as if the travel experiences only existed if they had been recorded. To preserve one's life by photographing it leads many people to a rather distant pictorial reproduction of reality – perhaps at the cost of recounting in words the tastes, smells and sounds which only verbal descriptions can give. But who has time to listen, or, for that matter to tell a story?

Souvenirs as coat hangers for memories

The ability of photos to make something visible is also to do with the materialization of travel memories. By looking round our own homes from just this perspective many of us discover things that are tangible examples from our own journeys through life. These memories are often manifested as miniaturizations of famous places. The little model of the fishing boat from the Canary Islands which I bought in the fish market is placed on the television. A ten-centimetre high folk costume from Singapore is placed in a frame in the hall. The godess of freedom and the Twin Towers stand as half-forgotten ash trays in the kitchen cupboard. A seven-branched candlestick from Jerusalem offers a kind of condensation of a memory. We experience the great via the small, the past via the present. Souvenirs become what Orvar Löfgren calls memories' coat hangers. Because they are three-dimensional they create a completely different manifestation from either photos or stories.

Similarly there is an *evocative* side to souvenirs. Precisely because they have no other function than laying down memories they contain a particular power. Their 'thingness' means that they can be arranged and re-arranged in our homes. Souvenirs are often aesthetically trivial or banal. But similarly they are a fetish, a piece of nostalgia, a thing without practical value. The task of souvenirs is to be aids to story telling. The outward journeys are cemented permanently into the memory via tangible objects. To look at travel souvenirs is to prolong the holiday and extend the experience.

Chapter Four

STAYING AT HOME – HOW COOL IS THAT?

The constant moaning about how boring Sweden is

Spring is on its way. Lectures in medium-sized Swedish towns. I am sitting watching the people in the square. Some are selling Bingo lotto tickets, there is a boy wearing rubber boots and a mint green track suit and a man with a plastic bag from one of the supermarkets on his cycle handlebars. A couple of businessmen are standing chatting by a kiosk. It is quiet and peaceful here. The man from the parks' department is wearing a bright yellow sweater with reflectors on. He is picking up litter: a bottle, a chewing gum packet and some old gloves which are lying in the slush. It is an ordinary weekday in an ordinary Swedish town. This is what I love, the apparently ordinary, the obviously commonplace.

This is Sweden. Until now I have mostly been reflecting on where we are travelling to. Home again I ask the same questions of the social scientists and anthropologists. This time instead I wonder what it is we want to get away from?

There are recurring statements about the Swedish mentality, our national character. Researchers call them stereotypes or cultural constructions of 'Swedishness'. Of course one must be extremely suspicious about such terms – not least against the background of the last decades of increased travel and when approximately one million out of nine million Swedes come from immigrant backgrounds. When we reflect in this chapter about what we are travel-

ling *from* it is obvious that simplifications will arise. But a
typical Swedish trait seems to be that Swedes often look
down on their own nationality. In comparison with people
from other countries, we are unusually interested in how
foreigners see us.

Conversations at Arlanda or other airports such as: 'At
last we can throw off the yoke!' or 'Now we are on our way
to real life!', witness both to a tendency to idealize other
countries and to undervalue one's own. One reason to
travel abroad could be the desire to avoid something that is
often heard in descriptions of the Swedish mentality from
both immigrants and visiting foreigners – and even Swedes
themselves: the inbuilt boringness.

Perhaps travel is one way of seeking contrasts; to be able
to stay for a few weeks or months in an environment where
'the yoke' doesn't get in the way. To dance the night away
by the warm Mediterranean, to live in a way that would not
be possible at home, to engage in discussions at the tops of
our voices with a complete stranger in a café in Seville
makes it possible for us to show another side of ourselves –
the non-Swedish.

However, it is obvious that we don't only travel to get
away. In a *supermercado* in Gran Canaria there are shelves
of Swedish goods such as crispbreads, soft whey-cheese and
Gevalia coffee.

Am I so happy to be Swedish?[1]

The perception of particular Swedish traits is based on the
observations of foreign visitors, on the judgements of immi-

[1.] Translator's note: 'Am I so happy to be Swedish?' This is a reference
to a song 'Jag är så glad att jag är svensk' (I am so happy that I am
Swedish), written by Paul Nilsson (1866–1951), priest and hymn writer.
He was not only very proud of being Swedish but also of coming from
the county of Västergötland. The above is a very jingoistic, patriotic song
which is nowadays usually only quoted ironically. Opposite is a loose
translation of the first verse:

grants as well as comparative cultural sociological studies. This means that if certain traits 'stand out' it does not mean that there will not be some people who *differ* from this behaviour.

To put it more directly: there is clearly an almost self-tormenting streak in the image of Swedishness. Perhaps this is built on the fact that many people from different countries express themselves positively when it is a question of Sweden's natural beauty, the cleanliness, good working conditions, excellent educational opportunities and good housing, but they become significantly more negative when discussing Swedes themselves. But even when Swedes themselves are describing their own typical traits the same words come up: distant and reserved.

Many Swedes spend more time listening than they do speaking themselves and this is considered by many other cultures to point to the fact that the person in question is 'self-satisfied' – something which is not in tune with the Swedes' view of themselves. In countries with a strongly stratified hierarchy it is not usual for superiors to converse with inferiors or to mix with them socially. This means that the Swedes' reticence or custom of avoiding conversation is taken as a feeling of superiority. In actual fact the Swede is probably just feeling uncomfortable, feeling that he has nothing to say in a spontaneous conversational situation. This could perhaps be when crushed into a lift, or arriving at the beginning of a party when they do not know anyone. Many Swedes are even said to walk round the block one extra time rather than have to travel in the lift with their neighbours. Forced intimacy is sometimes considered to be really painful.

This can also be said about Swedish punctuality. Not to arrive in time means in Sweden that one does not respect the lives of others or it is seen as a sign of general slovenliness.

'I am so happy to be Swedish.
What other country did God create that is so light in the summer with such clear starry skies as the wide beaches of Sweden?'

Many Swedes therefore plan their diaries by deciding both the start and finish time of meetings; for example one starts at 10 a.m. and finishes at 1 p.m. Then there is another meeting at 2.00 p.m. which lasts until 4.20 p.m. Just the idea of 'finishing on time' can be seen in other countries as impractical, unbending or quite simply unsympathetic. When a Swedish person meets this lax attitude in others it can at first seem charming, but often Scandinavians become madly irritated at having to wait in confused queues which often lead in the wrong direction.

This formal and controlled mentality is difficult to rid oneself of. Therefore to abandon one's calm on demand during a holiday and instead to act in a lively and temperamental fashion would only feel ludicrous. Perhaps that is why so many Swedes hate enforced high spirits. They hide rather than be called up onto a stage where they may have to be 'spontaneous' on demand. They would do anything rather than 'let themselves go'. They flee from the pig roast's artificial spontaneity.

At the same time, Swedes can be attracted by their own opposites, by precisely those personality traits which they do not have themselves. Obviously the personality traits of other nations are often romanticized – the irascible temperament of the Italians, the happy Danes' simple-minded attitude to cigarettes and alcohol, or the Americans' great self-confidence.

A guilty conscience about having a good time

Travel often means avoiding responsibility and routine. There is a clear contrast in Sweden between everyday burdens and leisure pursuits. Work is in some way more serious or more real than leisure time: 'No, now we must pull ourselves together and get something done.' This means that high spirits, the sensual enjoyment must certainly not be rejected but must be kept under strict control. This applies to childhood, holidays, free time – when everything else (important) has been dealt with. There is little wonder that many people never get round to engaging with real life or can even imagine that there will be an opportunity to do so in the future. It is no wonder that travel offers a relaxation which they cannot allow themselves at home.

Perhaps this has something to do with Swedish melancholy. What many foreigners and immigrants have observed is a lack of spontaneity and simple *joie de vivre,* despite the fact that everyone seems to work conscientiously in order to achieve a good standard of living. Take for example the word 'no'. In Sweden sentences frequently start with the word 'no'. When the time edges near midnight after a dinner party someone will say: 'No, now it's time to thank you for a lovely evening and say goodnight.' Or if a coffee break goes on a bit too long: 'No, now it's time to get back to work – duty calls.' Or, 'No, listen let's take a break now.' Or perhaps even more often: 'No, how nice.'

One way of explaining this constant use of the word 'no' is that it proves a hidden sense of guilt over having things too easy. Our conscience is about to prick and then it is time to say 'No, now we really must get on with things', or 'No, now I must go to bed.' The 'no' is evidence of an invisible dialogue. The 'no' presupposes two parties, two wills: one for and one against.

It was long considered sinful and is still barely thought of as respectable, to let oneself go with intoxication, sensual enjoyments or to consciously strive for indolence. In parts of the Protestant inheritance there is an axiom; man is weighed down with guilt and not released from it. In that connection, 'the natural state' is negative. Suffering is more legitimate than joy. According to Luther man is never satisfied as he can never successfully fulfil the law. His inner being is full of guilt. Then enjoyment of life becomes both a dangerous and immoral condition. This can be heard in expressions such as it is only when one has 'done one's duty' that one has the right to 'allow oneself' some time off. This creates a feeling that one is surprisingly thankful for good moments. Many have the feeling that there is a latent threat behind this – good things don't last, it is a blessing to have a good time. 'There will be a punishment soon, now that I am having such a wonderful time on this warm beach and for so long. Soon something terrible will happen.'

For many people it is therefore work that make's their lives seem worthwhile: to be useful gives happiness and meaning, to *do* is more important than to *be*. Work lies at the centre of identity – Scandinavians learn very early to talk about 'what they do'. But the emphasis on work rather than enjoyment means that the cleft between working life and leisure has become so sharp that people rarely 'enjoy' their jobs. On the other hand leisure time is actually threatening for those who have become used to work being the centre of their lives. For many it is a relief to be back at work and remain in their cells after a period of leisure time. This decreases the inner guilt, work keeps depression at bay. 'What would I do if I couldn't have a rough time of it.'

This means that irresponsibility finds poor soil in the Protestant world's work ethic. Physical enjoyment of life is something one can only allow oneself if one has earned it. One must somehow earn leisure in order to enjoy it. Talk of the permission to be idle highlights one of the 'most forbidden things' – of taking advantage of life; that intensely vibrant life. And they do this willingly on holiday. That is when they can at last really live, where there are vivid experiences. But they do not last.

The averted gaze

Perhaps the fabled Swedish shyness is about eye contact. Socially inadequate people are distinguished by the fact that they cannot look their contacts in the eye. Instead they look out of the window. Only when passing do they hazard a quick glance into the other person's eyes.

In this respect also, Swedes differ from people in other countries. The cultural anthropologist, Åke Daun, tells us about an American woman who went in to see her future boss, who was Swedish. The woman was sitting with a window behind her. The boss looked at her at the beginning of the conversation but then as he was discussing things with her he looked straight past her over her shoulder to the garden outside. He kept this up for so long that she automatically turned round several times to look to see what was so interesting in the garden. Daun drew the conclusion that Swedes tolerate and expect a lot less eye contact than Greeks for example. A recent immigrant to Sweden said to Åke Daun: 'Why do Swedes rarely look me in the eye? Is there something wrong with me?'

In certain cultures it is considered 'insolent' to look a superior in the eyes. The lowered glance is a sign of inferiority, one places oneself lower in a hidden hierarchy. Observed from outside it looks as if there are a great many Swedes who *start* from a position of inferiority, as if they do not feel completely worthy or are easily ashamed of themselves. This submission is clearly pronounced in the very Swedish custom of thanking at every available opportunity. It states in many guide books to Sweden that visitors must thank their hosts over and over again otherwise they will be offended: 'Always say thanks, thanks, thanks. Swedes prefer it two or three times.' This constant thanking, that one must say thank you in so many ways – the unspoken obligation to say thank you after a meal or the ancient Swedish tradition of 'thanking for the previous occasion', seems just as curious in other countries as the strange custom of saying 'Thank you for the conversation.' 'Thank you for your trouble.' The conscientious sending of thank you cards is witness to the fact that in some way one has been the recipient of a *favour*. Isn't *joie de vivre* or enjoyment something that one does not have a right to?

Avoiding other people – on the desire to be independent

When one travels on the Continent, not to mention the Asiatic countries, it occurs to one that as a member of a collective, a group, family or clan, everyone is expected to stick together like putty. The Swedish mentality often has an obviously opposite ideal – self-reliance. Here there is a long tradition of the strength of standing on one's own two feet and that this is the ideal – perhaps a remnant of the time when the farmer was forced out into a cold and desolate pioneer country. We all know the Swedish sayings 'Solitude is Strength', and 'Do things for yourself.' This strong desire for independence means that many Swedes go to extraordinary lengths to avoid being in debt to anyone. They cannot take too long before inviting someone again. They prefer to pay for themselves when eating in restaurants with friends and will happily discuss the bill in the minutest detail so that they are not indebted to anyone for anything.

One gets the impression that for many people it would be preferable to avoid all contact with unknown people. Many seek out their own patch. Even on a beach holiday on an island in the Atlantic Scandinavians will carefully mark out their own patch with a towel, preferring to lie in a corner or seeking out a deserted beach. It is only in the nuclear family that they can relax.

A typical example is the story that a couple of Spanish businessmen who came to a town in the centre of Sweden one beautiful summer evening. They checked into their hotel and then went out to see where the action was. Empty streets everywhere. A few cars were parked in one street, dogs barked. A complete small town idyll, it was eight o'clock in the evening but where was everyone? The obligatory pizza restaurant was closed for the summer. The town was devoid of life. Only a motor mower could be heard in the distance. The men became uneasy and went back to their hotel – but they had only been given a key in an envelope because the hotel staff had left the hotel lobby unmanned. Desperately they rang the police and wondered if there had been a catastrophe or an accident or if war had been declared. A joke perhaps – but it could have happened.

Why this longing for solitude? Perhaps because it offers a relief from the duties of social interaction. There is among many Scandinavians a deep satisfaction in sitting alone with a fishing rod, rambling alone in a forest or moor or in taking long walks with the dog. This is not the modern person's constant rubbing along with other people.

But how this desire for self-determination is fulfilled is partly a class phenomenon. A great many people go on camping holidays. Instead of sitting alone in a cottage or sailing with a few chosen friends, they are crushed together with other groups for several weeks in caravan parks or cottage villages where there is close contact with other people. Perhaps on holiday they are seeking an antidote to the monotony of work. But even if the ideal of self-determination is connected to certain social strata, it also seems to exist in the overflowing camping sites. If they could have afforded it many of these people would also have preferred to holiday in peace and quiet and to have had a cottage by the sea but for financial reasons they are forced into collective relaxation.

Nature offers a respite from enforced intimacy. Demands fall away. The Nordic interest in nature is said – according to the statistician and author Gustav Sundbärg – quite simply to be an antithesis to the Swedes' lack of interest in people.

Many feel that man should submit himself to nature's restful sounds, there he should be silent and listen to bird song and the sighing of the wind. For an urbane central European who would sooner see nature as something exotic – something that one passes by on the way to other densely populated areas – the Swedes' romantic experiences of nature seem remarkable. When one picks berries or sits by a forest lake with a fishing rod, it is then that many experience nature speaking to them. The individual carries on a wordless dialogue with nature. Quite simply nature becomes a place of reflection. 'In nature many feel as unstressed or unhurried as if they were out with a dog,' writes Åke Daun. There is therefore a sort of poetry in solitude, as long as it is not permanent or forced, especially solitude in nature. In nature there is a sweetness combined with melancholy. There is a lot of this in Swedish folklore, in music, art and literature. It is like a prayer rising from nature – its focus in a melancholy but strong longing. Many sociological studies show that nature is thought to offer a private religiosity.

> I have longed for home for eight long years,
> I have even felt longing in my sleep.
> I long for home. I long for it wherever I go
> – but not for people. I miss the earth
> I miss the stones where I played as a child.
> *Verner von Heidenstam*

In one way then nature is closer to a Swede's being than collectives or communities – which the urbane cultures in the south take for granted. The forest and wild open spaces are considered as a more honest state than communities or noisy parties.

Is there really strength in solitude?

How can we understand this constant striving for self-reliance? There have been a great many suggestions. One recent explanation has been that a typically Swedish ideal of childrearing is that a child should learn from an early age to look after itself. To be independent is desirable. Children are accustomed to early separation from their parents. Many researchers maintain that this leads to many Swedes learning at an early age that to be dependent is unacceptable.

But many Nordic inhabitants with this 'Strength in Solitude' ideal deny their longing for company. They keep a stiff upper lip and hide their feelings behind a mask of self-reliance. Children's leisure centres have as their aim to 'support a child's liberation from a close reliance on adults'. Children have to struggle on their own to tie their shoe laces or put their boots on in the cloakrooms of nurseries whilst their parents wait indefinitely. 'A child's ability to look after itself has become an ever more important question,' states the ethnologist Jonas Frykman. Similarly Havamal's words are more relevant than ever: 'People are what make other people happy!' Other people, community and friendship – but even the courage to enter into dependency on another person – remain basic and important life qualities.

In many other cultures the generations live in close proximity with one another, the acceptance of the obvious dependence on other people creates a security and closeness – that can sometimes be suffocating.

Let's not argue – on conflict avoidance

Conflict avoidance is yet another trait which is cited as part of the Swedish mentality. It means that many people go to extraordinary lengths rather than come into confrontation with people with whom they strongly disagree. In a conversation with friends it is more likely for one of them to change the subject than to enter into a discussion of subjects that they might disagree on. They reply evasively or without conviction. They will often go against their own opinions and agree – just to keep the peace. The cultural Swedish code – conflict avoidance at any price – is well known but difficult for others to understand. In all this can be found a kind of Swedish matter-of-factness, the usual conversational topics are the weather or the passage of time, what they are going to do, have done or intend to do. They even tell people when they are going to the toilet.

Here it is worth thinking of the English words 'agree' and 'accept'. In other cultures where one can see the point in drawing out differences of opinion, without despising or thinking badly of the person who does not share one's own position, the Scandinavians have a greater tendency to take a differing opinion as a personal criticism. But the words 'I don't agree with you' do not necessarily mean 'You are stupid or unintelligent'. Whilst an Englishman can criticize a suggestion with the words 'Damned nonsense!' – without it being taken as a slight on the person's integrity or honesty – a Swede would be deeply hurt by such a reply. The objective Swede thinks that his opinions are a part of his personality. A typical response is 'It is not worth discussing that as we think so differently.' In many other cultures it would be considered that this is the whole point of a discussion. A meeting or conference is not an exercise in choral speaking. Another statement is: 'Well that's what I think and you can think what you like and then that's the end of it.' It is not like this in conversational culture, where one consciously *seeks out* differences and where one even willingly constructs criticism against an accepted point of view with the intention of testing how sound it is.

Susan Sontag sees the Swedish reasonableness as deeply unhappy. She is openly critical and thinks that Swedes do not want to engage in conflict as they have too many inhibitions, anxieties and suppressed feelings. She believes that controlling their anger and avoiding confrontation leads to passivity and a kind of spinelessness. She is also certain that it is not because of the constant need for workers that people rarely are given the sack in Sweden however badly they carry out their jobs. Most Swedes would rather continue to employ incompetent personnel than lay themselves open to unpleasantness by speaking seriously to someone, and risk hurting their feelings or exposing themselves to hostility.

In contrast there are cultures where conflicts are not at all laden with anxiety, but rather an integrated part of a social life: arguments with staff, rows with noisy neighbours, rows with the butcher who sells tough meat, or the waitress who serves tepid soup or a mother-in-law who is forever interfering.

Gustav Sundbärg, one of the earliest twentieth-century writers to portray the Swedish mentality, writes: 'The Swede is never interested in *studying* other people. Try this in company: never join in the slander of a person who is disliked, that just would not do; never join in if others are praising a popular person to the skies that will be followed by similarly inarticulate agreement. But try, calmly and impartially, something more intimate: *analyse* a person's character – someone who is know to everyone in the company – try to find both his good and bad sides and how one could explain their relationship to each other. Without doubt the result would be complete silence from everybody, and after a few moments someone in the company would take up another subject of conversation.'

In Sweden a host prefers to sit dinner party guests next to people with whom they have something in common in order to facilitate conversation. In many other countries it would be the opposite, so that interesting opinions and personality clashes can arise.

On embarrassment about spirituality

Many Swedes will start to perspire and feel uncomfortable if the discussion turns to religious or spiritual questions. Swedish matter-of-factness is now applied to such previously taboo subjects as sexuality and eroticism. Fewer people nowadays will flinch from discussing everything from oral sex, gays' and lesbians' rights to adopt children, or the significance of a rich sex life. In light of this, Swedes' reluctance to discuss spiritual questions is all the more remarkable.

From being a relatively homogenous people, who more or less automatically accepted some type of Christianity, many have developed a personalized religiosity where one of the more important characteristics is: 'I am religious, but in my own way.' However, this spirituality is often connected to the deep reverence that we have seen Scandinavians feel when close to nature and the silent wide open spaces. Special occasions are celebrated by a forest lake or alone in a sailing boat. But when it comes to the more radical question – if there *really* is anything beyond the mountains – or if the entire religious world of the imagination is only a grandiose fantasy – many people keep quiet. Perhaps this can also be seen as a result of shyness; no-one wants to expose their innermost thoughts, they would prefer to keep their spiritual thoughts to themselves, but is there strength in being alone even at such moments?

Chapter Five

THE SPINNING COMPASS – INTERMEZZO

On confusion, homelessness and the purpose of life

We now leave the sun loungers, jet planes and journeys to more or less exotic places. We abandon the questions about our Swedish mentality. Instead I would like to make a journey into the ideological landscape which surrounds us. I will now discuss travel as a metaphor for the members of society.

Most road signs have been removed; old well-marked paths have become overgrown. But the cry for strong leadership and signposts speaks – admittedly indirectly but loudly – for the fact that man today belongs to a generation which is spinning about in confusion. In a society where political party programmes play an ever smaller role and the religious symbols appear to have lost their powers of interpretation, a type of vertigo has arisen.

Sometimes the present has been characterized precisely as *a-topical*, like a culture without a centre. Fifty years ago the majority of people travelled relatively safely through their life cycle, the alternatives were relatively few and simple. Previously people took a political stance and then lived their whole lives with allegiance to the same party. Choice of careers and religious beliefs ran in the family. This fairly homogenous society has nowadays been replaced by a selection of completely disparate lifestyles. There are fewer reference points. They have become negotiable. Nothing seems to be permanent any more but constantly changing.

But, in a world where there is nothing that is considered better or worse, no maps to rely on – no mental GPS system – that is when a feeling of homelessness arises.

One way (among others) of interpreting the increased interest in travel and the hunt for diversion is to see them as a flight from this kind of homelessness. A trip away from oneself, the centrifugal force that we discussed earlier, is helped along by a strongly intensified and polished culture. But perhaps modern man wishes neither to get away nor reach a destination. The most important thing is to ensure that one *keeps in motion*. Possibly one of the driving forces behind the desire to travel is the inbuilt anxiety that we are born with and which no technical achievements can suppress. We risk coming into contact with this anxiety if we slow down and slacken our pace.

The popular talk of 'seizing the day' – living in the present – can at first seem a tempting strategy. But the intensive interest in 'now' – in packing as much as possible into every moment – could be interpreted as a sign of the inability to devote oneself to a long-term project, to set goals and then patiently strive to realize them. Perhaps the present interest in enjoyment, food, golf and the culture of slowness is a sign of de-ideologizing, narcissism and a decreased tendency to take responsibility for anyone apart from oneself. Satisfaction appears more tempting now that the moral beacons of communal welfare have been extinguished.

Apparently more and more people are reluctant to take on long-term commitments. Fewer wish to 'box themselves in'. They do not want to be confined to one place, nor to dedicate their lives to a single calling, nor swear allegiance or loyalty to anyone or anything. It is more important not to mortgage their futures – 'something much more fun might come along!' But neither do they want to let the present be burdened by the past. In short, the present is cut off at both ends; the present is divorced from history. But to abolish history leads one to replace it with a commonplace accumulation of instant moments. It becomes a constantly repeating present. All this seems pleasant – in the beginning. But when the watchword changes to 'Everything at once' the risk of burn-out increases – or rather, superficial burning.

Flexibility and integration are the current bywords rather than opposition and integrity. Many people change their clothes several times a day. Others change opinions without embarrassment. But to be constantly ready for change drains one's energy. Many seem to tread water over a dizzy insight – which everything is changing. Because of this they cannot seize hold of their lives.

When much that has been permanent evaporates – politically and religiously – and signposts paradoxically are mistrusted as much as they are consulted, ever more heavy burdens are placed on the individual person's thin shoulders. They themselves must construct a picture of who they are, build their own compasses and take themselves alone into the world. To create a unique identity has become a project in itself.

The vagabond – he who strays from the path

The vagabond or tramp was considered slightly dangerous during the rather well-trained modern epoch, according to the sociologist Zygmunt Bauman. The vagabond was anarchic and had no master. He fell outside bourgeois regulated laws. At the same time he had no specific goal, was fairly inoffensive and could not be controlled. The vagabond himself decided in which direction he wanted to go when he arrived at the crossroads. He did not make any decisions until he saw the road signs. To control the self-assured and individualistic wandering vagabond is more difficult than controlling tourists or pilgrims who have a specific goal in sight. The vagabond has no intention of *belonging*. He is a 'lonely rider'. For him it is important not to be too attached to one place. To foster his apartness, to strive actively to be always original means that all decisions are put off until later. The aim of the vagabond is to be on his way rather than to cultivate roots.

Previously there were few such wandering vagabonds whilst permanently settled folk were in the majority. In modern society it is almost the opposite. Many people who socially speaking are 'settled' wake up one morning and discover that life has eluded them. They no longer belong. The country, their jobs, politics, the church, customs – everything has changed: tidy streets have become ugly, factories have disappeared along with their jobs, knowledge has been transformed into ignorance, secure networks of personal contacts have collapsed, old associations seem to be eroding from within. Nowadays the vagabond is not travelling around because he cannot put down roots, but rather because there are so few places remaining where he can put them down. Now many of them point out that most of the people they meet are also vagabonds. The world is fast catching up with vagabonds. Bauman expresses it like this: 'The world is remaking itself to the vagabonds' standard.'

The *flâneur* – on the inability to commit

The *flâneur* or man-about-town looks at life as a series of episodes, a chain of events without history and consequences. To drift through life means that one watches things and people flowing past, but without any great engagement with them. The *flâneur*'s observations make other people into participants and actors in his own life story.

From a cultural-historical perspective one can observe how the *flâneur* kept a low profile in rural society and during the industrial age. Whilst 'normal' people were on their way to important meetings or to work, there were always some who *avoided* hard work and chose instead to live cheaply. They were both interesting and attractive exceptions. The *flâneurs* appear as actors in their own right. They do not want to become too close to those they meet along the way. The less emotional energy they invest in their fellow humans, the easier it becomes to move on.

According to Bauman, a new moral code can be detected: do not become too involved in people, things or ideas. You never know how long they will last. Above all: never put off satisfaction if you can help it. Anything you want, try to have it *now*, you never know if what you consider to be satisfying now will continue to be so!'

An example is the arcade, the type of shopping centre which appears in most towns. This has become a typical meeting place and a symbol for the idler's persona. Here meetings take place which never become more than short episodes. They are a collection of *'nows'* which have been ransomed from the past and the future.

The pilgrimage

As we have seen, the pilgrim imagines that an unseen reality exists which has made itself known in a given place. That is where he wishes to go. That is why it is important to travel to those places where the Holy or eternal have been made manifest or to some tangible place such as a church, a grave or a view. The more that people realize how short their lives are, that time is confused, the more important it is to bind themselves regularly to places where the Holy has manifested itself. The word religion stems from *religere* which means to join together. The pilgrim yearns for places which are suffused by a higher Being.

The major religions have often claimed that mankind is on a journey. At the time of the Old Testament, the Jews were forced to carry the tablets of the law with them and they celebrated religious ceremonies wherever they erected the tablets – the Tabernacle was raised. On their journey through life they carried a symbol of continuity, but at the same time they were on their way up to Jerusalem – the place where the holy presence dwelt. And it was written of Jesus that he called Himself 'The Way', the first Christians were called 'Those who were on the Way', Gautama Buddha left home and went on his way.

Metaphors for what people feel during this inner pilgrim-

age are often connected to the needs of the body such as
'thirst'. But the thirst that is spoken of here is of a spiritual
nature. It cannot be slaked except at some spiritual spring.
Another metaphor touches a person's need to be seen,
confirmed, and longed for. The Hebrew word for gaze *'ain*
also means the same as 'source' or 'spring'.

And I once again think of the gaze of the icon which I
carry with me in my pocket. However far one travels one
cannot escape from oneself. Similarly, in the presence of the
icon one is always in the presence of oneself, confirmed by
'the Other's' gaze. Or – to use another symbol – one can
slake one's thirst at the source of life.

Change in the spiritual territory

But how then has the spiritual territory changed? Western
thinking has long been influenced by the Christian idea that
a living reality called God has actively intervened in earthly
existence in the person of His son, Jesus Christ. Since the
Enlightenment – but even long before this – religions'
thoughts about metaphysical questions have always been
questioned. The talk of a holy and almighty God – a spiritual force which lies beyond mankind, inscrutable in its
power, but which guards mankind – lost its power and
legitimacy.

During the twentieth century strong opposing ideas were
developed. Through these people received new compasses
and directions. When the Christian message weakened one
could let oneself be directed towards two new 'holinesses'
which grew up: an outer and an inner.

An *outer* 'holiness' praised the political collective. The
mass of society – the people, masses or the nation – was
transformed to a mystical grandeur with rites and symbols,
correct teaching and dogmatic conflicts. The social contract
is more than the sum of the people who uphold it. But the
socialist projects which brought happiness to everyone,
fascist constructions which broke the back and Nazi
utopias, led to the greatest trauma of the century. All these

profane holinesses with their hagiographies and hymns had no greater convincing force at an individual level. When a work colleague died, when a child was run over or when one realized one's own frailty and bodily decline, what happened then?

Another group talked about the *inner* world as holy. One performed one's devotions in one's own soul. The antidote to anxiety of heart was said to reside in the hidden depths of the psyche. The Unknown became spiritual grandeur. Psychology became religion. The source of holiness was placed in what Tomas Tranströmer calls 'the indoors'. Freud was the first. He had many followers. The Unknown – the dark source from which everything human could be understood – attracted its own priests, catechesis and exegetes. Freud was read dogmatically. Psychoanalysts were imperceptibly turned into a profane priesthood which unlocked the hidden meaning of dreams. Certainly, psycho-analysis is, and has been, important as an aid to self-reflection, but theory building soon began to take on a life of its own. Man was not master in his own house but was controlled by unknown forces. To a large extent the century's psychologists have created a new interpreting system for the inner chambers of the soul, but without the metaphysical engagement of theology. A new system of symbols has grown up which comforts, informs, admonishes and warns. Here there is no need of talk about gods, or spiritual forces, no revelations or catechesis, churches or holy texts. Every night a new codex was written which was quickly obliterated if no-one noticed it. The symbols of dreams were said to witness to man's belonging to something else; the subconscious.

The distributors of internal holiness were professionalized. A cadre of professionals developed diagnoses and categories, personality models and institutions. A confused world searched for clarity about its own inner being.

However, when confronted with death and suffering, people are seldom comforted by knowing that their longing for atonement is a consequence of oedipal confusion and that their need of comfort has its roots in too early separation from maternal protection.

The collapse of profane holiness

Psychologists maintained previously and with certainty that in everyone's innermost being there slumbers a holy spring; the oft-praised subconscious.

Several generations have sought solace in the surrealist images produced in dreams. Or as hordes of characters in Woody Allen's films would say, 'I need my shrink'. The places that people went to in order to seek solace changed from lofty cathedrals to calm clinics and soft sofas. It is neither gods, spirits nor churches that will give man peace, but insight and knowledge about his lost childhood. Before the end of the century psychologizing had become akin to spirituality: 'Seek out your inner child and you will be healthy.'

⁊ᎨᏛᏕᏗ

The view of holiness has been radically altered during the twentieth century. God was declared dead by a developmentally optimistic, technically idealized and scientifically knowledgeable generation, but their faces were stretched up towards heaven. Holiness was dragged down to earth and hung up as society's banner or squeezed into the most secret places in the soul. The thought that God could be a god in his own right – not reduced to psychic or social forces – was practically forgotten. Perhaps this idea is on the way out.

The loss of the great holiness has given rise to sorrow. The vanished god has left behind a vacuum: 'Who are You who fills the world with your absence' sang Pär Lagerkvist. A cadre of authors, film makers and artists described this anxiety which arose when loneliness in the cosmos became apparent. I remember how those who travelled in the space ship *Aniara* in Harry Martinsson's poem, experienced the melancholy in 'frightening space', a forceful symbol of the earth which travels through the precipices of the cosmos with neither steering nor goal.

The inescapable questions

Many people fight shy of the most basal absurdity of existence: the reality of death and the fact that good things never last. But now and then life deflates their sense of security. Questions that have been buried resurface. They are eternal and cannot be filtered out with the help of rhetoric about good citizenship, logic or psychological models. The irrational and rational uncertainties remain: why do we exist if everything must perish? Why does evil appear to triumph? Why does suffering seem to strike at random? Why must one be parted from those one loves? Why does the stroke of the axe come from within? Is there a living God, a holiness which is something more than just my own wishful thinking, something more than a social contract or a physical function and why do good things never last? Truly the question of the existence of God – as a real power and not just a metaphor for fate – is now being asked with greater urgency.

Sociological concepts and psychologists' theoretical words which stream forth periodically shield them from the fundamental provocative thought that existence is transitory, that everything is only provisional and everything permanent will be extinguished. But the existential anxiety remains.

Religious faith has been a bond between people. It has stated that existence is not merely a consequence of chance, but that it has a centre, a divine source and goal. Humankind is not just a by-product of evolution, a consequence of an arbitrary leap in development, but a desire of a living Other, the one who is called God. At one time the biblical world was a cultural axiom. If nothing else as a basic concept to ponder over, to distance oneself from or to believe in. Life was believed by Christians to have been created by God. Every human being would one day return to God.

Perhaps we are seeing a return of spirituality. In all great cultures religion has been the administrator of these existential musings and given them voice. The symbols of religion, its rites and office holders have maintained that there is a *factual* counterbalance to the brutality of life's condition.

This Christian dialect of holiness is on its way to being discovered anew, now that the profane holiness has collapsed. The talk that the body of society should have a metaphysical character seems long sought after – there is any number of disillusioned Marxists. Psychology is beginning to give way as an existential interpreter and has over time been replaced by practical concrete biology – especially the theory of evolution. At the same time fifty percent of the population claim to have some kind of belief. Many find solace in nature, in friendship, music or a glass of wine in the company of good friends. But is this enough when the cold wind blows? These are the questions which are posed during the inner journey.

❦

It is now time to leave the all-embracing reasoning. Let us discuss the importance of making an inner journey: to be carried towards the source.

PART II

THE INNER JOURNEY

No, she said ... no, I no longer want to go further away ...
I want to go home, I want to go home to my real home!
Only I don't know where it is. I no longer know where I
belong. I think I have lost myself. I think I have sold my
soul.

Hjalmar Söderberg, *The Serious Game*

Stracciatella, fragola and *limone*

Dusk is falling in Rome as I and hordes of other tourists are
swept along the alleyways between the areas around the
Pantheon – one of the world's oldest preserved buildings
from antiquity – and Bernini's fountain a bit further on in
the Piazza Navona. There are only a few blocks between
them. The traffic is hectic; the din is deafening and the air
not particularly clear. Only as the evening progresses do I
resume my peaceful wandering which I find restful for the
soul. Rome's fast tempo subsides as I take myself past Via
del Corso. The evening draws me into the waiting calm,
which is found especially in the back streets. The warm day
has long been replaced by one of southern Europe's dark
black nights.

I gaze through a dusty shop window at some old books.
Inside, an elderly gentleman is sitting wearing a light grey
cardigan that is too small for him. The top of his head can
barely be seen above the piles of sun-bleached, French

leather book bindings and magazines from the Second World War. He has pushed his glasses up onto his forehead and is reading *Il Messaggero*. Between the book shelves I notice an upside down mountain bike. It is bright blue.

A few metres further on is another shop. Inside are designer armchairs in bright colours. Steel furniture and coarse fabrics which I see from the minute price labels cost astronomical prices. Elegance and refinement stream through the window. The ladies' shoes in the next shop – Rome appears to have thousands of shoe shops – are illuminated with minimal, but strong floodlights. The three-dimensional is accentuated. Goods often stand on small displays of glass or mirrors. In the next shop sits an elegant woman – obviously the owner. Cigarette smoke rises to the ceiling. She is talking quietly on the telephone in a pleasant alto voice, whilst carefully studying her nails.

A scooter comes whizzing down the pedestrian street weaving carefully past the pedestrians. It is ridden by a nun leaning back in the saddle. She has a dark red crash helmet on over her black veil. She then stops and turns off the engine. A little dog hops out of her bag onto the pavement. They disappear into a *gelateria*. A slight whiff of petrol fumes hangs in the air.

There are ice cream parlours virtually every fifty metres here in the centre. Long gleaming metal benches with fruit ice creams in bright colours and strong flavours. People sit in rows in front of the marble counters and await their turn. I order my usual mixture: *stracciatella*, *fragola* and *limone*. The nun orders a caffè macchiato.

On the troubled heart

How does an inner journey begin? Perhaps like this: many of us have a desire to do something *real* with our lives. We do not just want to waste our time in a passive and egocentric manner, letting days come and go. Sometimes we feel an inner poverty and think: 'Is there nothing more to life?' But at the same time we have nothing that particularly weighs us down. Suddenly we feel alone; a cold feeling of desolation makes itself felt. In these circumstances some of us think that we should involve ourselves in *something else*. But we never get round to it.

Such aching desires can come over us at any time and anywhere. It may happen when we are off on our travels or when we are at home sitting on a well-worn settee. Often we can experience a strong need to re-evaluate our lives – reinvent ourselves – when we stand at the crossroads of two stages in our lives.

When we enter a new phase of our lives we often wish to take stock; to take a compass bearing. We do not want merely to drift along without taking command. But how to go about it? Some people seek a professional counsellor, a spiritual adviser or a psychotherapist. Others write letters to themselves or start a diary. Yet more sit for hours discussing things with friends. Others purchase a last minute flight: 'I must get away and think!' But their goals are the same, to make some kind of re-evaluation of their situation, what could be called a mental diagnosis.

The attempts to establish one's own position 'Where am I now and where am I heading?' are important at different stages; when young people want to leave home, when a student is confronted with the dizzying alternatives on offer and must *choose* (and even more importantly – discard), when life rushes by at full gallop with childcare, work and a more-or-less routine marriage. The feeling exists in the underlying anxiety of middle age when life's melancholy hangs like a mist – despite good friends and a comfortable lifestyle. And it exists at the beginning of ageing when we realize how few years we have left and we are happy that we have not yet started having aches and pains. At the point of transition between two life stages we seem to be carefully drawn in towards our own inner being.

At other times people do not so easily slip away from the existential fundamental questions. Then they are threateningly near. A person has done something that they bitterly regret. Another has experienced being left by a loved one. A third hears from their doctor that a tumour is gradually spreading throughout their body. At such times people are more or less brutally aware of life's underlying tragedy. Questions about meaning and goals, the illusion of freedom and the inflexibility of death cannot be ignored or put off. We cannot say: 'I'll take care of the spiritual side later.'

Put another way: Now and then people feel the touch of homelessness, what Hjalmar Söderberg calls *'the troubled heart'*. These feelings cannot always be explained in terms of an unhappy childhood, an intolerable work situation, social isolation or alienation. It comes from within. Inbuilt in the human condition there is something unsettling.

I have previously said that one way (among many) of interpreting the intense interest for life 'on the move'- both geographically and mentally – could be the need to avoid a confrontation with one's own troubled heart. In the flight from themselves people rush restlessly through their lives with neither map nor compass. But the insight into the inescapable things of life – time, death and freedom – is an essential precondition of the inner journey. Therefore taking time out is just as important as reflection or taking stock.

Many people have ambivalent feelings when asked to perform such inner journeys – 'Ugh, let's talk about something more light hearted!' certainly some people talk with enthusiasm about going on a retreat and living a monastic life for a few days. Others dream of painting water colours on an Atlantic island or turning the TV off for a few months to devote themselves to modern Spanish lyrics or taking a renewed interest in Swedish history. But unconsciously they make sure that they never have the time for these activities. The inner conflict is obvious.

But in the long term it is not possible to escape from anxiety of heart by frenetically seeking entertainment, working obsessively, or through power, education or the desire to remain young. Neither do powerful cultural or spiritual experiences help – except briefly. Many discover to their surprise, that anxiety of heart cannot be cured by either the beauty of nature, from reading novels, lighting candles, incense or through listening to Bach's music in the twilight.

Religion and literature, not to mention psychology are full of 'signposts'. The scope is enormous, everything from Ignatius of Loyola's *Spiritual Exercises,* Dante's *Divina Commedia,* to Jung's individualization process.

What follows in this section of the book is the description of a personal journey. I do not aim to connect to any given 'charts' even if its basic structure is close to classical Christian mysticism. I have placed this *story of an inner journey* in three popular tourist destinations in Europe – Rome, Paris and Venice. But the central theme is not just these three places – but the inner process that I wish to illustrate: in Rome, reflection and friendship, in Paris beauty and feelings and in Venice the paradoxical experience of being seen in the midst of a confused existence. Neither should these 'stages' be seen as steps which lead a person ever nearer to the ultimate meaning of existence. Various stages merge into one another.

To mistrust one's feelings

Let us first make a short summary. As we shall soon see, large parts of the spiritual traditions are sceptical about the fixing of experiences that we have mentioned before. The inner pilgrimage does not depend on something as fleeting as man's feelings. Instead, people must break away from themselves, achieve what many religious mystics call the 'death of the self'. Only he who loses interest in himself achieves peace. The ability to give is more important than the ability to receive. Surrender is more important than self-fulfilment. But in order to give of oneself, one must *have* a self to give – autonomy – not just experience one's self as a social construction, but instead see oneself as responsible and free.

The journey is about something that lies *beyond* the individual's need to 'feel'. The chase after spiritual experiences is alluring. But if a person ignores themselves and instead reaches out to others, they attain secret insight. It is often wordless. It becomes trivial if it is spoken aloud. Carefully the person is led through an inner darkness. There they have inexplicably, but clearly, a feeling that they are in the hands of something greater.

> Those who cannot exist anywhere except on their facades
> Those who are never absent minded. Those who never open
> the wrong door and catch a glimpse of the Unidentified One
> – walk past them!
>
> Tomas Tranströmer, from 'Golden Wasp',
> *For the living and the dead*

In order to achieve this, sooner or later a person passes through a night where they are forced to *ignore* their need of understanding, experiencing and achieving. Ancient psychology should speak of something which lies beyond thought, feelings and will. This is not the same as intellectual resignation, lethargic laziness or dogmatic credulity. It is rather an insight into both the basic secret of the human condition and existence.

A prerequisite for the inner journey is a paradox: only *he who forgets himself for the sake of others will find himself*. But consciously to strive to avoid self-absorption, to think of the needs of others rather than one's own is not given much attention in today's individualistic culture. In 'Love yourself' books and in virtually every book on popular psychology there is an absence of talk of *the needs of others* or that in fact people need other people, that there is a certain courage needed to be able to let oneself go for another's sake, that dependency can also be for the good. Goodness, gentleness and humility are often noticeable by their absence. It is first and foremost the self that is elevated. But self-absorption (which is not the same as a stable self-confidence), remains a basic hindrance to personal growth. The serious attempt to forget oneself and instead to open oneself up to the real needs of others constitutes an unnoticed but well-trodden path to a rich inner life.

I think of the prayer of St Francis of Assisi: 'Lord, help me not so much seek to be consoled but to console, to love not to be loved. For it is by giving that one receives and by forgiving that we are forgiven, by losing our lives we find them. It is through death that we rise to eternal life.'

But we are in Rome, let us go out into the warmth of late summer.

ROME IN LATE SUMMER – ON THE IMPORTANCE OF KNOWING WHERE YOU ARE

Is this where you are? If it is not, go to where you are. I will wait for you there.
Engraved in the floor at Gardermoen Airport in Oslo

On not wandering aimlessly hither and thither

Lido di Ostia

One day I take myself off to the railway station. It is early morning and the air is still fresh. But the thermometer is already creeping up towards thirty degrees and I long for the sea. The afternoon is going to be unbearably hot if I do not get out of the city centre. People are hugging the shade under the enormous white roof of the Stazione Termini. Finally I find the right platform.

Soon I am sitting on a train looking out over the reddish-brown landscape. We pass station yards with their railway carriages covered in graffiti. We pass heavy industrial areas and finally reach the Mediterranean on the horizon. Out here along the enormous newly built beach promenade of Lido di Ostia there is a mild warm wind blowing. Squinting against the sun I observe an armada of sailing boats. There is obviously a race in progress.

'*Aranciata, Birra, Coca-Cola, Acqua minerale, Acqua naturale!*' shouts a man walking along the hot sea shore. He is carrying a tray in front of him. Young boys with dark brown skin and sun-bleached hair sell pieces of coconut.

First I walk onto the hot stones and look out towards the hissing groundswell.

Lido di Ostia. Directly north of here lies the Porta di Roma. Rome's harbour town during antiquity is situated a short distance away. The sand is glowing warmly under my feet. I carefully keep to the boards which have been laid onto the white sand. The waving plastic streamers of the parasols glitter against the water. People are dozing in the sun, smothered in sunscreen factor nine. The sellers walk nonchalantly barefoot along the edge of the beach. They are bedecked with plastic belts, bags, imitation watches and scarves. In each hand they clutch a collection of sunglasses. Sometimes they stop and spread out a mat and set out their goods. No-one seems to sell anything.

Lido di Ostia. I am not at all certain if the philosopher Seneca or other giants from antiquity have been here – but it is very likely. The great travellers, both in the outer and inner sense, not least that great Doctor of the Church, Augustine, took leave of his mother at this very spot. The year was AD 387.

All those antique philosophers, aren't they hackneyed?
About ten miles behind me lies the Eternal City. Here, they have all lived; the great thinkers such as Cicero, Seneca, Augustine and Marcus Aurelius.

Sometimes their writings seem inaccessible. One notices among the writings of antiquity an insufferable elitism. Remote patriarchal attitudes become obvious – not to mention a barely disguised contempt for weakness. But at the same time; the problems of anachronism are clear, we attribute to the ancient thinkers attitudes which they did not hold at all, since we are influenced by the attitudes of our own time.

∽◎∾

Long before the blinking of the Internet and the hectic ringing of mobile phones, long before the all-singing all-dancing post-modern talk about a frenetic ever-rushing generation, the antique traditions pointed to the journey that each person had to embark upon; the journey into oneself. Often the great names of antiquity have presented us with maxims, clearly defined in their simplicity and clarity.

There is one thing they all have in common; they speak of the importance of nurturing an inner life; of living intensively and not allowing oneself to be deceived by the 'myth of later'. In the middle of what one has left behind and what is to come one must live one's life – perhaps a banality, but well known in the phrase *carpe diem* (seize the day!) or *age quod agis* (do what you do!). Seneca, in particular, often uses travel metaphors to describe the search for an authentic life.

Seneca is important in our context. Born about the same time as Christ in Cordoba, Spain he came early to Rome and there received training in rhetoric and listened to lectures. Around AD 32 he became questor, the first stage in a career as a government official. Under Caligula (who was Caesar from AD 37–41) Seneca became famous as a noted orator. However, this made Caesar so jealous that he condemned Seneca to death. Caligula called Seneca's oratory 'sand without use' – it was impossible to build with. Claudius Caesar's wife Messalina exiled him to Corsica. On the island he wrote, among other things, the text that we shall soon examine more closely, *De brevitate vitae,* 'On the shortness of life'. It is in this book that we see how Seneca compares life's journey to a voyage across the sea.

Seneca engages with the most private thing of all: himself. He writes about the necessity of taking command of one's own life. The idlers' and vagabonds' unstable lifestyles are in the end devastating. Why? Because in this way a person becomes passive, a victim of circumstances. Instead, Seneca emphasizes that each person must guard the freedom zone. Responsibility is the nucleus of identity. To put off the meeting with oneself permanently leads primarily to self-delusion.

This is how it would sound in contemporary language:

One lives as if one were never going to die; one never thinks of one's corruptibility. One allows time to be wasted, as if one had unlimited access to it, during the very day which could very well be one's last on this earth. You can hear most people reason like this: 'When I reach fifty I will wind down a bit and take things more calmly and quietly.' Aren't you ashamed of not spending the last half of your life in self-improvement? To take time out to improve your soul (*yes, that is indeed how he writes!*) only in the time, which is not allocated for any other activity. Is it not a bit late to begin to live one's life just as it is reaching its end? What stupid forgetfulness of death's inevitability it is, to leave the only important thing until the fiftieth or sixtieth year and to start to live one's real life at the age that few people reach.

Knowing where you are

'Most people have no precise goal but drift, easily swayed, for ever dissatisfied, from one place to another ... They drift hither and thither just as a wave on the ocean floor continues to move even after the storm has passed, and they never achieve any respite from their desires ... But you have not condescended to look into yourself, to listen to your soul for one moment.'

Seneca appears to reason thus:

The basic prerequisite for an inner journey is that a person ceases all activity and takes a bearing. In order to start this journey they must know *who* they are, *where they are now* and *where they are heading*. If a person never thinks of his life as directed *towards* something, but drifts aimlessly – letting the days pass – then he will eventually make a bitter discovery. That he has never actually lived. Other people's commands or his own sudden inner impulses have decided for him.

... One thinks, that with few exceptions, life passes us by whilst we are still preparing to live ... No, we do not have too little time allotted to us, but we waste too much of it ... One person may be mastered by an insatiable avarice, another may fawn upon someone and give themselves continual stress by completely unnecessary work, a third may drown in floods of wine, a fourth may loaf about inactively the whole time, another may rush about and exhaust themselves with ambition and another travel through every ocean and country in their hunt for gain.

I squint over my pocket book out towards the sea. There is a fresh wind blowing, the heat is slightly less tiresome. On board a large ocean liner the crew are trying to unfurl the mainsail. Large motor boats with gigantic outboard motors fly forward across the high waves. Far out on the horizon several oil tankers are anchored. Their profiles are gigantic. And I read in Seneca of the risk of being tossed through life like a rudderless vessel.

> You have therefore no reason to doubt, that the person who has white hair or a wrinkled visage has therefore lived a long life. It is not said, that he has lived long, he has merely been around for a long time. Think about it! Consider that, if the man had been on a long sea voyage, and right after his leaving the harbour he was overcome by a violent storm, which tossed him here and there through the violence of opposite winds, and round in circles in the same waters. Such a person has not undertaken a long voyage but has been tossed at length on the waves.

On inner integrity

Yes, certainly there is an irritating, slightly haughty individualism, sometimes even an arrogant condescending tone in a lot of Seneca's writings. But at the same time he is adamant that every person must find their *own* way, and not chase after the approval of the crowd. They must carve out their *own* vocation even if they are sometimes forced to take a contrary course. They should seek their own way, their own individuality. But that which our early twenty-first-century's fashionable philosophy would create as a confusing myth about an authentic ego is completely ignored by this high-minded old gentleman. Just listen to this!

But as long as we roam here and there without following any signposts, but only the discordant shouts and cries which call us in opposite directions, our lives will be wasted on fruitless diversions and seem to us too short even if we work day and night to achieve our goals. Let us therefore clearly keep in sight both the goals we wish to achieve and the way we have to go ... Here it is not like other wanderings: then one has several signposts to keep to and one can ask the way of other people, without the risk of going astray; but here it is completely the opposite: the broadest and most well-travelled route is here the most difficult ... One should therefore ask oneself, which is the best way to proceed rather than the easiest.

And I think that in this there lies a hidden elitism. Why should the majority always be wrong? Similarly, an individual's identity is personal, never collective. A distinct sense of self, a clearly defined person who is certain about their own journey and strives to realize it is not the same as an egocentric or an egoist. The search to realize one's vocation cannot be the same thing as self-absorption. On the contrary, it is the opposite. A stable identity is a prerequisite for deep intellectual fellowship. Mature people are those who neither anxiously cling to others nor desperately try to flee from intimacy. Paradoxically enough, it is only those who *have* an identity who can forget themselves – for the sake of others – and thereby find themselves.

Or as Seneca would say: 'A prerequisite for an inner journey is attention to oneself, not least to those tendencies for restlessness or for always hunting after something new. The problem is that man both wants to and avoids meeting himself. But he neither perceives this fundamental duality in himself if he never puts down roots and looks around to ask where he is, and where he is going.'

A lifestyle which consists of constantly rushing around in circles can be treacherous. The traveller thinks that he is being carried forward. In actual fact he is only going round in circles. In his eagerness to be everywhere he has never taken part in anything at all. But it is certainly not a drone-like existence that Seneca is referring to:

> I do not exhort you to a lazy and unproductive leisure,
> neither to sink all your energies in lethargic and sensual
> pleasure which the vast majority of people are so enamoured
> with, that is not what I mean by settling down to a quiet life.
> You should certainly find tasks, more meaningful that all
> the labours you have hitherto carried out with such energy
> ... But nevertheless, believe me, it is better to take stock of
> one's own life's accounts rather than that of the granary.

To caulk the vessel of one's soul[1]

Across to the left from the place where I am sitting, I see an
old boat wharf: grey-haired fishermen with skin like dark
brown leather and rows of white teeth are standing about.
They are discussing an upturned boat. It has cracks in its
hull. The tar and paint have flaked away. No-one seems to
have bothered scraping it for decades. They are pointing to
the boat's dark floor, looking at each other and then out to
sea. I am too far away to hear what they are saying. The
sound is absorbed by the din of the sea. They continue
discussing and shaking their heads. Many of the boats lying
in the wharf are half-rotten. If anyone should turn them
over and put out to sea in them they would immediately
take in water and sink. According to Seneca this is exactly
what happens to those who never give themselves time to
collect themselves, create an overview and caulk the hulls of
their own souls.

   The boat itself – the personality – should be so stable and
permanent that it copes with both periods of storm and
calm. If we interpret Seneca's reasoning it would sound
something like this: Man should create a personal history
for himself by identifying important events in his life, and
creating an integral part of his memory bank. This can be
done by keeping a diary, making sketches or checking

[1.] Translator's note: The correct translation of the Swedish is 'To caulk
the vessel of one's soul': we would take this to mean 'strengthening the
soul's defences'.

photographs of important life events and in this way accommodating in his life a larger completeness, or by talking to a confidante. In modern fashionable parlance this is called narrative psychology.

The consequences of such self-evaluation of who one is and how one became the person that one has become, is that it creates a core of integrity. In the co-ordinating story of one's own life appears something unique which *only I* have been part of. During the last century a whole professional body has evolved whose task it is to create a secure framework for such life-story telling; we call them psychotherapists. But actually one does not need professionals in order to discover and put words to one's own life history – rather good friends who are prepared to listen.

The person who is constantly searching has finally neither the energy nor the ability to slacken their pace, make an evaluation nor sort out their memories. There are therefore treacherous consequences if there is not a sound 'hull' in the vessel of the soul: everything they have taken part in will run right through the leaky bottom planks.

No, no, say the postmodernists of our own time. Even a person's ego is under constant change – without centre and periphery. There is no permanent basis either in the inner world of the psyche or in society at large. The self is nothing more than a social construction. Every time a person recounts his own life history he creates a new version of himself, everything is fluid. This postmodern position is against Seneca's beliefs.

If there is no 'inner nucleus', a memory bank, which takes care of what a person experiences, one's impressions evaporate away and they live more and more in the tyranny of the present. It is important that the co-ordinated life story builds a framework or a heavy keel under 'the vessel of the soul'. Without history man has neither present nor future. Each person must be heard, allowed to tell their own story, or to follow Seneca:

Life can be divided into three periods: that which is, that

which is past and that which is to come. The moment that we live is short, the time that we will live is uncertain, that we already have lived is certain ... A soul which is free from anxiety and finds itself in equilibrium and with peace of mind can travel through all of life's passing phases. But the soul of a harrassed, driven person seems as if forced under a yoke, they cannot turn around and look back. Their lives have consequently trickled away into the deep, and in the same way that nothing can be gained, however much one patches it up , if there is no hull which takes up and preserves it, so it means nothing however much time one is granted, if there is nothing there, where a foothold can be found. It leaks out through the cracks and holes of the mind.

Life is reduced to

> ... several short and anxious moments for those who remem-ber nothing or know nothing of the past, whilst they waste the present and go in fear of what is to come. When they stand at the end, then they finally realize, all too late, that they have achieved nothing throughout their whole lives however busy they have been. As when they no longer have their usual busy-ness, they are nervous at their lack of activity and do not know how to use or to drag though the free moments. Therefore they eagerly seek out something new to occupy themselves with, and all the time which is passing in the midst of their various tasks they find unbearable.

Certainly he sounds surprisingly modern, our antique friend – Seneca.

Travel as a flight from oneself

Even Seneca was convinced that there are journeys that are more flights from oneself than the desire to discover new countries, places or views. The most important motive in this case is not what one is travelling *towards*, but what one is travelling *from*. The traveller himself may describe the journey as a sort of inquisitiveness, the joy of discovery or wanderlust, but on closer inspection it is more a case of restlessness.

Seneca, in one of his letters to Lucilius, quotes Socrates (470–399 BC) who was writing several hundred years earlier:

'Why are you surprised when your travels do not help you when you carry yourself with you? You are pursued by the same worries that drove you on your way.' What enjoyment can new countries give? Or the knowledge of other towns and places? Your restlessness has not taken you anywhere. If you want to know why this flight does not help you it is because you are fleeing together with yourself ...

You travel hither and thither in order to shake off a burden which is firmly attached, but which, because of your restlessness, becomes even more troublesome, just as a cargo influences a ship less so long as it is motionless, but when the ship is in motion, it shifts from one side to the other. Everything you do, you are doing against yourself, and you are hurting yourself with the actual motion because you are shaking a sick person.

I close the book, get up and walk along the pier. I can see some sailing boats racing in towards the shore. The wind has increased and there is a whistling through the rigging and flapping sails. A little way out is a buoy that all the boats must round before they beat into the wind and start tacking diagonally along the white sandy coast towards the town of Civitavecchia. It is fascinating to see the sailing boats in the strong wind working hard to pass the buoy. They are heeling over a great deal. In one little botched-together dinghy with only a thin centreboard beneath the boat (can it really be a *Flying Dutchman*?), one of the crew is hanging out towards the surface of the waves. The speed is fast. The larger ocean-going boats take the waves stiffly, rolling past the buoy – under the water they have heavy keels.

Indirectly Seneca reminds us of the burdens that people carry. They do not become any lighter because they are rushing about and trying to forget them. In Seneca's symbolic language they remain just like the cargo in the boat. There they slide about in the bottom of the boat and disrupt the voyage – life's journey – if they are not properly secured. One of these many burdens can be called the troubled heart.

Cultivating friendship

Villa Borghese, meetings and inner journeys

Once again I am back amid Rome's hectic noise; tourist buses force themselves past the Spanish Steps. People mill around Corso with heavy backpacks. On practically every park bench and in every restaurant there are people sitting writing postcards. I try to find a free seat in an Internet café but without success.

One evening I take myself up along the Via dei Condotti, and look into the Caffè Greco which is in the corner beneath the Spanish Steps. This place was started by a Greek, Nicolas della Maddalena. He sold Turkish coffee as a speciality as long ago as 1760. On the whole, most of the cultural giants have taken a coffee break here: Goethe, Heine, Schelling, Dickens, Wagner, Liszt, Beethoven, Grieg and our own Swedish Sergel, Gunnar Wennerberg and Prince Eugen. And across the road, Axel Munthe had his surgery for several years at the beginning of the twentieth century.

They sat here for hours near the Spanish Steps deep in discussion. The café was the local meeting place for Bohemians and artists. Many had their mail sent there. The waiters still wear dinner jackets. There are a mass of photographs hanging on the walls. But it is packed and warm. The velvet-covered red sofas are uncomfortable and it is expensive.

I am now standing opposite the Spanish Steps. Dusk comes slowly. The façades are illuminated. I hardly notice that there are street lights in the square. But in barely half and hour they will be completely obvious; first slightly light yellow, then they change to brown to finish with dark red. During this time more and more people collect beneath the wide steps. A caricature artist sits next to a gas lamp and draws a shy young Japanese who is sitting erect. The result creates sniggers from his friends. Men from Togo lay out blankets on the street. There they display bags, watches and copies of Gucci and Armani. They constantly look around so that they can quickly gather up their booty if a policeman should appear.

But I go up the Steps, turn to the left up the hill towards Via Trinita del Monte and stop for a while in front of one of the large oaks in front of the Villa Medici. Here there is an extraordinary fountain. A stream of water gushes out of a cannonball. This exact cannonball, so it is said, struck the large iron gate of the Villa Medici. The right-hand side of the gate still bears the indentation. The marksman was said to be Queen Kristina of Sweden, who it is claimed fired it from the ridge over by the Castel San Angelo, all because her good friend, Cardinal Azzolino, who at that time lived here in the Villa Medici, had not come to see her at the prearranged time. Probably a tall story.

A little bit further on from the Villa Medici I stop above the rushing traffic and look down towards the Porta del Popolo. It was through this gate that Kristina rode when she denounced the Swedish crown in 1654. But I ignore the history of the place and return to the park of the Villa Borghese and walk along Viale del Bambini. There is a little restaurant under the giant oaks – La Casina del L'Orologio – where the customers, if they get there in time, can sit in hammocks. I have sat here every time I have visited Rome. Soon I too am swinging in a hammock. I look down at my computer's blue-white screen and start writing. Every now and then I look around. Over several evenings I have noticed two different couples who have returned to these leisurely swaying seats. One couple is a pair of young lovers. The other is two elderly gentlemen who sit here every evening holding long and intense discussions.

The lovers sit entwined with each other. Yesterday their hands were in motion. Their love is intense, their embraces nearly aggressive. This evening they are mostly drinking in each other's eyes. Obviously they are head over heels in love with each other. No, of course; I know nothing about them. Perhaps I am writing more about myself than about them.

A little way off sits the other couple. Elderly Roman gentlemen with a hint of stubble, blue shirts and dark jackets. One has a yellow tie, the other a pale mauve one. Cigarette packets on the table. They wear light brown shoes and socks of good quality. Carefully creased. Elegance and grey hair. They have plastic bags on the table. Every now and then they take a book out of the bags. They discuss them intently in quiet voices. Sometimes the conversation stops for a few minutes. Then they stare out into the distance over the square. They speak slowly, occasionally sharing a joke. With them there is no noisy neurotic conversation. Periods of silence. Even about these I know nothing more concrete. But these two gentlemen remind me of yet another reason for an inner journey – friendship.

To be respected as a unique person

Many of the learned writers from antiquity praised friendship as a means of reaching an inner core – this is true of Seneca as well as Cicero. Let us listen to Seneca again:

> Nothing is as favourable for the soul as a steadfast and inner friendship. Is it not good when you have faithful hearts to which you can safely entrust every secret, whose knowledge of your situation you have no need to fear, whose conversation can calm your anxieties, whose utterances can help you to come to a decision, whose encouragement can banish the clouds in your mind and whose very presence brings you happiness?
>
> ... Most important of all you should beware of pessimists, who view everything with a gloomy mien no matter what occurs, and with whom nothing is free from complaint. It may be, that such people could be faithful and mean well; a companion who is always upset and complains about everything is, however, an enemy to what we are seeking, namely peace for the soul.

But the one who is always smiling at me, who always agrees with me and in every way possible flatters my conceitedness – is he really a friend? Someone who acts in a hypocritical manner, false and flattering. More than a hundred years before Seneca, Cicero wrote:

> One must consider that nothing is more likely to ruin friendship than obsequiousness, flattery and ingratiation. Such people ought to be marked with every conceivable appellation; this belongs to characterless and false people who say anything to please others and nothing for the sake of truth.

Francesco Alberoni, Professor of Sociology in Milan, is an author who in our own time has discussed how friendship differs from love or infatuation. He does this in the spirit of Seneca and Cicero. Alberoni thinks that a *friend* is neither a teacher who instructs, a lawyer who judges, nor a partner who always needs us. No:

> The first desire of friendship is the freedom of the other person ... Friends must not teach each other how to live nor try to improve each other ... They must not force each other to do anything ... If, for example, a friend has done us a favour, we are grateful but we avoid asking him why he has done this. A friend has no need to give explanations and one does well not to ask for any. One should not analyse his behaviour to try to discover his motives. A friend's actions should quite simply be free actions.

According to Alberoni friendship is something which marks us out as unique and unmistakable *individuals*. We place great emphasis on a friend's judgement because a friend is someone who understands. But the friend is not a judge who gives trophies or prizes, he does not hand out any certificates. Instead the friend helps us to develop our own authentic individuality. This compares with Seneca's and Cicero's speeches on the need to seek one's own style and to ignore trends.

Alberoni's point is that friendship is a relationship

between two independent individuals. Other types of relationship are often built on the needs of one party being met by the services of the other. So we tend to turn to another person if we are in distress but these situations do not create friendship. On the contrary such cases can give rise to discord and misunderstanding. Friendship cannot endure if we make ourselves dependent on another. Instead, friendship is incompatible with strong need as this leads to an imbalance of power or the need for gratitude.

> If I consequently turn to a certain friend I am in the end dependent on him, I give him power, a power which increases the more I put myself in his hands. This behaviour goes against the sovereignty of friendship and leads unavoidably to its demise ... We have made him see our friendship as a burden. Friendship must always be easy ... Friendship is an incidental gift not constant charity.

The signs of friendship

Alberoni attempts to characterize various types of relations. *Acquaintances* he calls those people who are so close to us that we know what they think and what their likes are. We know them, we help them and vice versa. In short we have a good relationship with them. But we have no deeper confidence in them and do not tell them of our innermost thoughts. Another type of relationship is one which is part of a *collective solidarity*. These are, for example, work colleagues or those with whom we share some sort of ideology, a faith and convictions or who fight for the same ideals as we do. We have permanent ties to them. It is mostly for practical and pragmatic reasons that we have ties to them. The third type of relationship is that which can be found in specific *role situations* – between neighbours or between employers and employees. These are based on need principles; one gives and takes according to fixed rules. In all these forms of relationship are found sympathy and good intentions. Here there are people whom we like, whom we help and support and who in their turn help and support us.

But the word *friendship* Alberoni reserves for the type of person one feels completely relaxed with, where there is trust, happiness, inquisitiveness and familiarity: 'A friend is someone who finds comfort in wishing another person well and who sees that these feelings are reciprocated.' Friends are quite simply people whom we like and who like us, but have no desire for ownership. To experience that type of friendship is a kind of grace.

When I look over at the constantly embracing lovers I look for the place in Alberoni's writings where he shows how friendship is different from being in love in several important ways. Yes, here it is:

> Love is something which has a definite beginning, ... a flash of lightening, an apparition. On the other hand friendship arises not through an initial manifestation but over a series of successive meetings ... Love is a passion, an *ardour* . In passion there is always suffering ... Friendship detests suffering and avoids it as much as possible. I can fall in love with someone without my love being reciprocated, but my love does not cease because of that. Love is not mutual ... but strives to be so.

On the other hand one seeks out friends because one wishes to have fun with them – to put it in banal terms. Friendship cannot endure in an atmosphere of too high appreciation. Flattery is devastating. In friendship we expect the other person to have more or less the same opinion about us as we ourselves have. But praise destroys friendship. Paying attention to, cultivating and maintaining friendship is important from the perspective of the inner journey.

The spontaneous meeting
The mild evening has given place to night. The lovers have left. Others have sat in their seats. Some families with children converse endlessly whilst a white-haired gentleman – obviously the grandfather – accompanies the children on the swings. No-one seems to mind the lateness of the hour. The laughter of the children echoes along the alleyways.

The two elderly gentlemen are still sitting in the same place and gesticulating even more. Is that their second or third bottle of wine, I wonder, whilst I continue to leaf through Alberoni's text.

It is sometimes said that friendship grows slowly. But this is incorrect according to Alberoni. We do not become friends with people we associate with most frequently. Instead we can just as easily consider someone a friend even if we have only met once or twice and if they live a long way from us, just because we have a good time together. We feel completely relaxed and listened to. We are inspired to show the truest side of ourselves when we feel secure – and not judged.

Friendship is thought to arise when we feel empathy with someone – a kind of immediate friendship, according to Alberoni. It starts a bit at a time, drop by drop, with meetings each one of which refers to a previous meeting. Even if we meet a friend again after a long absence it is as if we have only been apart for a few moments. We can take up our conversation again precisely where we left off. But what really amazes us is that our conversation never stops with subjects that we discussed at an earlier meeting. Each meeting is different, we discover new avenues. Silence is not threatening.

Meetings between friends create moments of strong intensity. They create times when we realize something about ourselves and about life that we hardly realized that we knew. A good conversation contributes to a sort of continual description of a situation. During the meeting we feel that the other person helps us to think of things more clearly ourselves. We can feel this even though we may not have the same opinions.

Meetings between friends are like 'corn buried in time'. Whatever happens *between* meetings seems to be virtually unimportant. This separates friendship from love, work solidarity and being in love. After a meeting with a friend we do not feel that intensive need – 'We must see each other again!' No, both are well aware that the conversation between friends has been meaningful, but does not give rise to any exaggerated desire to prolong the conversation indefinitely. Both parties realize that the meeting by its nature must be discontinuous. This of course does not mean that one does not wish to meet one's friend again. On the contrary. But friendship's feeling of need only occurs if one actively wishes to regulate the unregulatible. Force destroys it.

Why are conversations between good friends so important? Well, according to Alberoni, they convey moments of genuineness, the disorganized person receives some meaning, the versatile person receives some pattern for their lives. During a good conversation one can get a feeling that everything belongs together. When one is listened to one is permitted to relate one's life story. Or in the words of Seneca – 'caulk the vessel of one's soul'. Each and every one of us is a whirlwind of desires around a nucleus of glowing fire. But at meetings with friends we can touch upon our innermost feelings. 'By talking to a friend I discover what I really am, for I am only myself in relation to that which I think that I can be.'

In a similar way to Seneca maintaining the importance of 'caulking the vessel of one's soul' by creating one's own history for oneself, Alberoni writes about the role of friendship for this inner journey: 'To tell something is to think out loud. The friend is always a deliverer; he inspires us to an honest, objective search. It is we ourselves who judge, it is by ourselves that we find the way.'

Nothing is so alien to friendship than that it is transformed into teacher-pupil or admired-admirer. A friend is not a guru. Friends do not give or receive instruction. Friends are not spiritual guides, pastors or path finders but remain fellow travellers.

The multi-faceted structure of friendship

The first thing that happens with acquaintances is that they often fill up all the gaps. They say practically automatically: 'What have you done since we last met?' With this question they are trying to fill an empty space in the passage of time. They say: 'Where are you going on holiday?' It is the time line – forwards and backwards – which is under the magnifying glass. Acquaintances talk about the weather, how it has been or what it is going to be, either positively or negatively, what they have done or are going to do.

When someone meets a friend after a long time it is however as if they have never been parted. Everything has changed, new problems and masses of things have happened, but despite this they have a feeling that they are continuing with something that they were in the process of. It is as if time has stood still.

Friends who meet – even after a few years – do not overwhelm each other with questions about what the other person has been doing. To recreate the past day by day is not in the friends' interest. The past does not seem to interest them at all. Instead they start talking about what is closest to their hearts at the moment. Alberoni expresses it even more crudely: people who say 'Now you must tell me about everything' or 'Now I want to know everything' are not real friends. The one who says: 'I haven't heard from you for ages, you could at least have written!' is not a real friend either. A friend just asks: 'How are you? Are you well?' The only thing that interests him is that we have a pleasant time, here and now.

This means that friendship's time in Alberoni's terms is *granular*. Friendship's time consists of a series of now-moments, whilst a lover's time is more tight, coherent and intensive. Lovers talk for hours about what they have done or what they intend to do. Loves want to reconstruct the past and look forward, they aim for fusion; to go up into the other.

Friends do not meet in order to create a new unit – like love's 'now we are no longer two but one' – something which raises itself above them both. They have no wish to change each other or to grow together. Each one instead follows their own life's course, their personal destiny. Each one seeks their own happiness and love. Friends can be found beside us in this search, stand at our sides and help us, but they are not the goal of our search.

But is Alberoni not exaggerating? In a relationship with one's friends does one not now and again talk about the past and the future? It is in this case always on our own personal past or our own future as individuals. What is always left out is the past and future of the *friendship itself*. That is something that is taken for granted – a kind of gift of grace. We would bore each other to tears is we discussed our past as friends. And even worse would be to worry about the history of our friendship. Lovers are worried and anxious – as there is a matter of possession in the situation. 'Friendship's existence is found in the granular structure of time and cannot survive if this is changed.'

Swimming against the tide

San Clemente and the ugly word 'character-building'

The sun is unrelentingly hot. One afternoon I sit for a while opposite the Colosseum. I place myself so that I can look over towards the Palatine and the Capitoline hills, two of the ancient hills that Rome is built on. Here, under one of the parasols in the restaurant Osteria al Gladiatores, there is a pleasant shade. I order two cold *aranciata* and think: how can anyone survive in this climate?

Trams pass regularly in front of me. Diagonally down on the left I glimpse the Titus arch. In front of it are hordes of Americans in sun hats. They are being photographed – one at a time. Droning hot buses of shiny steel stand in the background. Folk flee into its air-conditioned interior. This triumphal arch was built by the Emperor Domitian in the year AD 81 – all to the memory of Titus's exploits in Jerusalem in AD 70. A little while ago I noticed on the inside of the triumphal arch several reliefs which show the booty seized from the Jews: among other things the seven-branched candlesticks, the tablets of the law and a pair of silver trumpets. Where these spoils of war have disappeared to, still puzzles researchers. The Vandals plundered Rome.

In the Jewish Talmud it states that everything disappeared to the bottom of the Tiber as long ago as the fifth century. But who knows?

I finish my drink and continue along the busy street, Via di San Giovanni in Laterano. One rarely notices the little church which immediately appears to the left – San Clemente. It is a remarkable place. When one walks into the building one passes physically through several layers of history. Three churches are built above one another. A long way below can be heard the faint sound of running water.

When I enter the uppermost church I see a beautiful mosaic which was created in the twelfth century. It is contemporary with the more famous mosaic in Ravenna. The motifs are unusual: a large black cross which is imbedded in a beautiful pattern of leaves. The cross itself is of wood. In this sparkling, colourful yellowy-green scene I discover birds of every kind, small animals and masses of flowers. Several everyday scenes are depicted with great care. In the midst of the greenery I see a couple of well-known figures. One of the Fathers of the Church, Augustine, is caught amongst the flowers. Pope Gregory we will soon get to know. Just in front of this dark green and gold mosaic I see it again – the face – the gaze of the icon.

⁘

When I go down a flight of stairs I find yet another church. This was built in the fourth century and consists of a nave on which the upper church is built. Even here there are a number of frescoes – but it is difficult to see what they represent. At the bottom of the left aisle of this underground church a narrow stairway leads yet deeper underground. The air is damp and it is badly lit. If I listen carefully I can hear the sound of water. It is a gentle murmur from an underground watercourse. I climb into the remains of a Temple of Mithras from the third century. On the wall there is a picture of the god Mithras killing a bull, but also a picture of the sun god. Down here, explains the guide, there was also a dwelling which belong to Clement. He was a distinguished man from the first century who became a Christian and offered his house to be used for religious services. In all likelihood the apostle Peter has been here and perhaps even Paul.

In the space of several minutes I have wandered through several thousand years. Deep underground I meet people and ideas which I have previously only read about in heavy tomes borrowed from the library. The whole of Rome is full of the physical evidence of things that have long since disappeared. The past is tangible. Far-off thoughts become insistent. Jung would definitely say that we have passed from the conscious over the unconscious down to the collective archetypical symbols, all in an area as large as a normal country church in Sweden.

Then I walk back along the Via Imperiali and take myself up to the Capitoline Hill. In the middle of the square is a bronze statue of Emperor Marcus Aurelius (AD 121–180) For a long time people thought that this statue represented the Christian Emperor Constantine. This saved the statue from destruction. It was only a long time afterwards that people realized that it represented Marcus Aurelius. Michelangelo – who together with Bernini – pops up all over Rome, designed this beautiful square where I am now standing. The bronze statue is placed in the middle of an oval patterned stone mosaic. Because the plinth is so low, it is easy to see the statue. The horse's belly is disproportionately large. Marcus Aurelius's gaze is directed straight forward. He looks stern. Marcus Aurelius is also akin in his thoughts to Seneca and Cicero.

Marcus Aurelius returns to the idea that man must cultivate his originality and reflect on his own potential freedom from circumstances. He wrote meditations – stylized notes. His point is that things are subordinate to people and that one can even distance oneself from suffering. The important thing is not what one's situation is, but how one deals with it – to trivialize this stoic philosopher on a horse. Man must make himself free in his own inner being. That it is not an outer form of freedom that they are talking of and that even a slave such as Epiktetos considered himself a free man. Even in an emperor's palace with all its routines and compulsions, one could consider oneself free, according to Marcus Aurelius. But to achieve this freedom, insight and will are needed. His point is that man can train his character.

When I read this I get cold feet and think that such heroic ideals sound far too harsh. At the same time his ideal of freedom is close to Dostoevsky's who, in the *Brothers Karamazov* lets the starets Zosima say:

> The world has proclaimed freedom, especially in recent times, and what does their freedom mean? Simply and solely slavery and self wasting! For the world says: 'If you have needs, you must satisfy them, for you have just as much right to do so as the leaders and the rich have. Do not be afraid to satisfy them, you can even increase them.' This is the message in the world today. In this one can also see freedom ... 'But the way to the correct and true freedom,' continues Zosima, is 'the vows of a monk, fasting and prayer.'

In contrast to the freedom which satisfies the need for experiences – preferably as quickly as possible, the freedom that Marcus Aurelius speaks of can only be achieved by privation, this popular word of little value. Freedom must be won; man is not born to it. It must be worked for, it is not owned. It is not a freedom which exists outside us, but is an inner freedom. It is dependent on a change in a person. Through such a virtue a person develops a strong character. In Marcus Aurelius's thoughts there is a term which has long been misunderstood and which is completely unfashionable at the beginning of the twenty-first century: 'character-building'.

But when I see Aurelius' sharp look, his courage and resounding quotations – I wonder what happens to all those who *cannot* cope, those who are unable to train their will, who fail in their resolutions that they are unable to carry out? What help is a heroic strength of will when it really counts? Is it not merely a refined version of cynicism's twelve stages of how to become a happier person? What about those of us who cannot cope with it despite all our intentions? Such questions remain, but this does not detract from the fact that Marcus Aurelius – in the same way as Seneca – has important things to teach us. Man should try to create a resistance to the state he finds himself in and develop an inner nucleus of integrity.

Finding one's individuality
Even Seneca was clear about the risk of pseudo-employment. He is very scathing about the self-absorbed academic:

> As far as I'm concerned such people, whose time is taken up by studying and publishing worthless knowledge, one can without fear of contradiction state that they have achieved nothing of any use during all their hard work. And of such people there are a great number of these even among Romans whose knowledge is of the sort that, if you keep it to yourself, does not enhance your private knowledge or happiness and if you communicate it to others, does not make you seem more learned – just more boring.

One person, who in this spirit, often refers to the great minds of antiquity, is the British author John Cowper Powys (1872–1963). Powys does not possess the ancients' pregnant language. On the contrary, he is seldom verbose and diffuse. But he has also in a decisive way emphasized the active resistance to standardization. He places part of the body of thought of antiquity into a modern urban environment:

> In a city it can actually seem, as if a super human strength of character is needed to avoid being dragged into the whirlwind of sensation seeking, which at every moment seethes round and about. When one considers the fact that written about and constantly repeated brutality damages the soul more, and vulgarises the spirit more coarsely than that

which we see in everyday life, and when one thinks of the
unimaginable mass of people who, every day feed their souls
with the illustrated weekly press and greedily soak up vulgar
comedies and unbelievably sentimental films, so one must
ponder over how, in such places there can be one single
human being left, whose chaotic inner life can preserve at
least a modicum of similarity with the inner life in former
times. Nothing other than extreme and practically misan-
thropic individualism can save us from this banal atmosphere of spiritual vulgarity.

This popular salvo of little value is fired off without embarrassment. Of course Powys is also rather annoying in his
extreme mistrust of the vulgar. But what he says is in tune
with Marcus Aurelius. Only he who swims against the tide
reaches the source. We listen to Powys again:

> What is important is that in the depths of each person's
> inner life there is a strong, bitter, resistant philosophy. It is
> this strength, this defiant resistant power within the depths
> of the soul, which gives every true shaping of the soul the
> steel and permanence that it needs for a person to be able to
> linger at the brutal, glittering surface of life without being
> fascinated or anaesthetized by it, but to listen to its metallic
> ring.

In the same way that a person greedily throws themselves
between several external places, there is a risk associated
with too much reading. Seneca writes to his friend Lucilius:

> Your letters and what I have heard of you have made me
> harbour good hopes about you : you do not rush about
> hither and thither and do not worry yourself by changing
> your place of residence. Such restlessness belongs to a sick
> mind: the first the most important proof of a calm soul I
> think, is if one can find a foothold and remain with oneself.
> But you must beware of one thing: that your reading of
> many authors and all types of books does not lead to a kind
> of fickleness and instability ... to be everywhere is to be
> nowhere. Those who live their lives travelling discover

finally a great deal of hospitality but no friendship: with necessity it goes the same way for those who do not concentrate on being faithful to a single author but skim them all in a terrific hurry.

Most important of all is for people to learn how to deflate self-important people's self-absorption, or rather to ignore them. They must avoid constant references to others that might be taken as learned or cultivated and instead develop their own reflections about what they hear or read. Powys writes thus:

> It is always a sign of an upstart in the world of culture, that he sharpens and polishes his sentences until they equate with the latest fashion within opinion forming. A cultured person, meanwhile goes his own way and does not bother about justifying himself to the world. Why should he worry about that? ... Half-educated people [that is how he writes] let their personal experiences and expertise be interfered with and flattened out by a slavish respect for modern science or conventional respect for traditional religion. The educated person takes both these dogmatic authorities with a pinch of salt ... for in a cultivated person's life intellectual snobbery has ceased to exist. He is not interested in the question of whether his attitude is 'intellectual' according to the current fashion or not ... Real culture has almost always a certain tendency to combine infinite subtlety with a kind of childish naivety
>
> One often has a feeling that a *merely* educated man holds his philosophical views as if they were so many pennies in his pocket. They are separate from his life (it is the same thing in the world of religion). Whereas with a cultured man there is no gap or lacuna between his opinions and his life.

Powys mixes banalities with accurate observations. He says among other things how important it is not to tire out one's brain on puzzles which in all likelihood are insoluble. All fine thought systems can founder in trivialities such as if a person has a stomach ache or has slept badly. Many afflictions can be cured by fresh air, a good walk and a stroll in the sun.

On the importance of deflating the over-confident
Powys addresses those people who, with feelings of power
and a certain feeling of superiority, maintain that they
know what is right and what is wrong. And he does it with
a furious force. One ought to poke fun at a know-it-all. It
is necessary to harbour doubts about all dogmatism and all
ready answers. In every activity there must be a necessary
perhaps. Every doctrinaire submission – that applies to
scientific theories, political ideologies as well as religious
symbol systems – must be questioned.

According to Powys:

> It is extremely healthy for our personal culture, if we, in this
> 'dialogue with mystery' were capable of understanding how
> one-sided and unsatisfactory all rational solutions to the
> mysteries of the world are. It is precisely here that the uncul-
> tivated but knowledgeable person feels irritated, confused
> and uncomprehending when faced with the true simplicity
> of childish mental development. For it seems, as if no scep-
> ticism goes far enough, before it has reached a point where
> virtually every mystical interpretation of existence seems
> more acceptable than one that is purely scientific.

This means that *ignorance* itself is a great blessing for the
person who starts on the journey of the personality culture
(the words that Powys usually uses). The fact that one has
come so far that one 'is not ashamed of one's ignorance,
especially in subjects that are in fashion at the moment and
in the latest aesthetic slogans, is a great achievement.' And
he continues in the same bombastic exaggerated style:

> Think for example of the difference between an eccentric old
> gentleman, who has discovered his own personal and origi-
> nal taste, the quintessence of his own mental life ... and all
> those whose moments of relaxation are filled with dissolv-
> able and confused fantasies, with the empty encyclopaedic
> souls, that one meets socially and whose eternal cackling
> about thousands of spiritual trifles are more soul destroying
> than the babbling ramblings of senile old men.

On the surface, it is the vulgar mass culture that Powys is criticizing – but obviously his thinking is influenced by the great mass ideologies of Nazism and fascism which engulfed Europe during the Second World War. It is blindingly obvious that Powys is suspicious of the whole idea of democracy and comes closer to the small number of cultural giants who desire and try to seek out *deep* knowledge in the most profound books.

But at the same time, in practically aphoristic form he formulates sentences in the spirit of Seneca when he emphasizes the significance of living in communion with nature, but without fastening oneself too firmly to anything. This means using the gifts of fortune but not being dependent on them. If we achieve that, the result is a kind of elevated position, a secure peace of the soul which is the true and unchangeable happiness and thereafter follows a happy and cheerful mood, which does not depend on external things but on inner harmony.

Trastevere in the evening

Late one evening when the day's heat has abated I pass the Via della Scrofa on my way to the Pantheon. I look up towards a picture of the Virgin Mary. It is dirty where it has been hanging on the wall of a house. Mary, with her head covered in a blue veil is sitting bent over her son. In the niche underneath the picture someone has put some fresh flowers. I cannot distinguish their colour in the darkness. Several schoolgirls cross themselves as they pass the picture of Mary. For a few moments they gaze intently up towards her. One of the girls closes her eyes for a few seconds. They then continue on their way. Obviously they all look into Mary's eyes. But Mary smiles inwardly.

Not far from the Piazza Navona I see a man sitting at a little table. On the table he has placed a lighted candle, several dice and some tarot cards. He yawns and waits for the next customer who wants to look into the future. In front of me stands the ancient building, preserved for two thousand years. The Pantheon was dedicated as a Christian church in 609 by Pope Boniface IV, after having been a temple dedicated to all the gods. The aperture up in the roof is nine metres wide. Legend has it that when the church was dedicated the devils went up with a shriek through the hole in the cupola.

I then sit for a while on a plastic chair with McDonalds written on it. Around me there is a lot of rubbish and striped drinking straws, several tourists from Wisconsin laugh out loud. In the square in front of me the beautiful people stroll past – clean lines, clean shoes, mobile phones and large ice creams. A little way off I can hear the sound of horses' hooves.

Later I take myself off to Corso Vittorio Emanuelle past the Piazza Campo di Fiori and look up at the statue of Giordano Bruno who was burnt at the stake here on 17 February 1600. His astronomical work threatened the biblical view of the world. I walk along the Tiber, over Ponte Sisto and turn off toward the old quarter around Trastevere. The alleyways are full of restaurants and the din from the kitchens can be heard in the square. But I creep into the church of Santa Maria in Trastevere.

Up there is a mosaic from 1148. It represents Christ as King of Heaven with his mother, Mary, at his side. The image is remarkably like the one on my own icon but there is a significant difference. Christ has his arm around his mother. Up in the arch the letters Alpha and Omega hang down from the Cross – symbols for the beginning and the end. If one looks carefully one can detect a little bird in a cage which is being let down from a cloud – perhaps an image of the incarnation, I think to myself, as I feel the little icon in my pocket.

Chapter Seven

PARIS IN LATE AUTUMN – ON CULTURE, IDEAS AND LONGING

If art was nothing more than a lengthening of life – would it be worth sacrificing oneself for? Is it not more illusory than that? The more I listened to the septet, the less I could think such a thing.

Marcel Proust, *The Prisoner*

The red bicycle

Paris. Early one autumn morning, several Quarters east of the Gare du Nord. I am staying at the home of an elderly lady who, regular as clockwork, goes out onto the balcony and smokes whilst giving her moth-eaten dog an airing. The window boxes are still resplendent with greenery turning to copper or deep red. I can hear the din of traffic down in the avenue. There is a chill in the air. After a too-sweet jam on my croissant and warm milk in the strong coffee I borrow her red 1950s bicycle. It is heavy and unwieldy in traffic.

The street cleaners are cleaning up the pavements and washing the streets. Waiters dry off the night's damp tables. Down on one of the barges on the Seine I can see a man standing on the deck taking a shower. Yesterday's washing is hanging out to dry. A puppy roams up and down the quayside, barking in an agitated way. When I have parked the bike against one of the town's rough walls I turn around. The red colour creates a contrast to the grey-black stone facades of the turn-of-the-century houses and dark green doors. If I squint, the cycle gleams like a splash of colour in an Impressionist painting. For a while now I have been staying in the city of *flâneurs*, dreamers, artists, Bohemians, philosophers, writers and lovers. For the first few days I give myself up to the idealized notions of the stereotypical picture. Beyond the din of traffic I can detect distant melodies on an accordion, Basques, easily creased jackets and tired faces. Surely it is the ghost of Toulouse-Lautrec. Just as I am squeezing past a swaying Polish tourist bus near the Opera I think that I glimpse the writer Albert Camus in the crowd. History lies dormant, as if beneath a thin membrane.

Later I pass the Pont des Artes. The sun breaks through and I am bathed in sunlight from the glare on the Seine. I see the soft dull greenery of the Vert Galant, the shadows under the trees on the Ile Saint Louis. Tourist boats glide past. They are like giant insects. Shiny windows mirror the sky. Skilfully they give way to the sleepy barges with skippers squinting in the bright light whilst standing at their giant tillers. Chairs have been put out along the alleys of the Luxembourg gardens. They look inviting. But I turn back towards the centre, cycle past the bourgeois discrete charms of the Café de Lilas and stop at a junction. I am looking for a CD by Charles Widor.

Yesterday evening the bars and outdoor restaurants were crammed packed down here on the West Bank. Around the entrance to the Metro in the Place Michelle people were standing in a circle listening to the street musicians from Jamaica – the entire square was swaying to the beat of reggae music. The waiters smashed crockery on the pavement in an attempt to encourage customers into a Greek restaurant. Today it is calmer here. The cafés are filling up with customers. The tourists gush forth like black lava to the Musée d'Orsay. Always these black clothes.

I park the cycle and talk to some elderly boutique owners. A skinny man with streaming eyes stands shivering in a long cardigan. He has thick glasses and the obligatory neckerchief from 1920s Europe. Daily papers from the

Second World War lie next to plastic wrapped green instruction books for computers from the 1980s. Clumsily folded maps of Buenos Aires are squashed between nineteenth-century wood cuts and Japanese comics.

The streets are dirty. Cascades of red neon fluorescent advertising signs offer everything from kebabs, cheap Internet services to concert tickets. My eyes wander. But when I look up I discover an unobtrusive charm. Above the shop window are well-worn ornamental window frames carved by strong hands about a hundred years ago, window frames with well balanced proportions. There one can see joy in craftsmanship – the quiet refinement of the architecture. Paris's back streets are peaceful. There one can hear the sound of heels against cobbles, a couple laughing out loud. A man stands leaning against a wall talking quietly into his mobile phone.

Paris is the home of cultural refinement. Of course, one can also find social misery here, the difficult situation of immigrants and degrading poverty, as in all large cities. But in the centre, practically speaking, every Quarter is impregnated with the philosophical brilliance of the centuries, revolutionary uprising, literary salons, the charms of the cafés and restaurants – not to mention the torment of the artists.

On this occasion I am looking for the Paris of beauty or culture – the places of pilgrimage for everyone who experiences culture as a relief from the brutality of life. Art and music give comfort against the 'unbearable lightness of being', relieve the anxiety of heart. Many come here because the city represents values that enrich them.

In Paris they made a name for themselves: the Impressionists, the Expressionists, Cubists, Existentialists, Pataphysicists and Dadaists. This is the home of the various 'isms'. Misunderstood American jazz musicians found acclaim here long before they were recognized in their native land. The third floor of the Museé d'Orsay is a place of pilgrimage for anyone who has Renoir paintings as posters on their kitchen walls.

I walk away along the Boulevard Saint Germain. Over there in the café Les Deux Magots the philosophers sat. Several Quarters away Giacometti hammered out his anorexic figures. Not far from the Arc de Triomphe is the Orthodox Church. That is where the exiled Russians found refuge during the Russian Revolution. The philosopher Berdjajev called attention to beauty as a religious virtue. As did Simone Weil – who spoke intensively about beauty as a route to a spiritual reality. But far beneath the tunnels of the Metro and fashionable Paris the traditions of the Middle Ages lie preserved. Universities, churches and buildings are witnesses to how beauty lives in symbiosis with spirituality. In church art, architecture, music and poetry the membranes between the aesthetic and the divine have been rent apart. In the halls of learning as well as in the meditative cloisters of the monastery we have been reminded of the spiritual significance of culture.

On culture as food for the inner journey

Let us return to our theme; the inner journey. If we in fact stop chasing round in pointless circles and no longer drift aimlessly, but steer a course across the sea, in modern parlance 'take control of our lives', then what happens? Yes, then it is not unusual for us to realize that we really have lived – but what *for* and *in what way*? We are now searching for more lasting values, rather than for things that are merely transitory. Family and friends, as well as fitness and health become more important. For some, nature becomes a holy place. There they feel as if they are part of something *Grander*.

Such values certainly do not need to be of a high cultural nature or particularly high flown – but a second step in the inner journey is taken when we actively search for the source which satisfies a deeper thirst. Obviously culture constitutes a source of life. How many people are there who take themselves to the world's concert stages? What enormous sums of money are spent, year in and year out, on performances, concerts, folk music, rock and opera? The queues wend their way to museum exhibitions around the world. Why do people do that? Perhaps because there is a 'need' which only art or culture can supply. People busy themselves regularly in the world of literature, staring into paperbacks. Others follow film, Hungarian prose or study Moorish art. Even in antiquity one heard of *ars longa – vita brevis*. Life is short, art endures.

But let us not be seduced, we must be careful! There is a haughty self-absorption in a lover of the arts where this type of name-dropping and parade of learning can leave a bad taste in the mouth. The snobbishness of the aesthete can be devastatingly egocentric and arrogant in its superiority. All such concealed or open arrogance must be carefully deflated. Erudition and cultural refinement have nothing to do with moral judgement, spiritual stature and even less with goodness. The highly educated person can be a malevolent villain; the intellectual giant can be a cynical full-blooded egotist. It is often the complete opposite. The person who has never read a book in his life or who has not the slightest idea about high culture can be an absolute saint.

For some it is culture itself that nurtures their inner lives. To read a book slowly which deeply moves them; with some difficulty to understand a Persian poet or to listen to the adagio in Schubert's string quartet, to study in detail turn of the century buildings or listen to the vibraphonist in a Modern Jazz Quartet or the saxophonist Ben Webster, to stroll for hours in a quiet art gallery or to read history – such things are the necessities of life; especially in the second half of life's cycle. The point is that they are seeking 'nourishment'. Or in the words of the Nobel Laureate, Joseph Brodsky: 'Aesthetics is the mother of ethics.'

To be more precise: when someone has calmed down and stopped worrying they discover a longing for something more tangible than the fleeting enjoyments of the present. The need for entertainment is replaced by the longing for something completely Other.

On the metro between Port Royal and Porte de Clignancourt

I am sitting on the Metro one day. She is sitting opposite me and has long frizzy hair. She looks as if she comes from southern Europe. She is reading a Swedish newspaper. After many years living in Sweden she speaks excellent Swedish but she is now back in Paris. When she discovers that I am interested in religion she talks at length, rapidly, and in a well-formulated manner:

> I'm not religious or anything, but the last few years I have felt such a restlessness. I tried all the New Age therapies that Stockholm had to offer. Yes, I suppose some might call me a seeker. When I was young I read Sartre, I was fascinated by his criticism of all great systems and his emphasis on the absolute solitariness in man's situation. But now I haven't the energy for the existentialists' talk about the absurd. Of course – I have now realised in retrospect that my questioning was a manifestation of some sort of mid-life crisis, a feeling that life was passing me by. I was confused about everything. What do you think, you who seem to know something about psycho-analysis?

Before I had even had time to realize that she was asking a question, she continued:

> So then I joined a group which took part in deep breathing therapy. I thought that was a bit weird, so I read Freud and Jung instead and discovered Poul Bjerre. There were several of us who met regularly at that time on the south side at the Café Pan. Is it still there? It was really nice there and we made a sort of inner journey into fantasy, we used various visualisation techniques. Once I was convinced that I had lived in a previous life. Reincarnation seemed completely plausible to me. But now I can even see through these 'new age' fads.

She continues, whilst she checks which station she must get off at,

Of course, I believe that those types of spiritual solutions can work for some people. I don't like people who grumble at us seekers just because they think they have already found the answers. All these fascinating systems and ready solutions seem so artificial in some way, they do nothing for me. It all became clear to me a couple of years ago when a friend of mine became seriously ill.

She talks forcefully and verbosely whilst the underground train glides forward on its rubber wheels.

I grit my teeth and listen to music instead. But now I've also started to think that all this high culture is just as meaningless. Of course, it is lovely to put on a CD sometimes – but when we ourselves die, what difference does it make that Mozart's music is beautiful. What use is beauty against tragedy? By the way, I expect you know that there is a violin concert in the Madeleine church tomorrow?'

We are standing on the platform at Château Rouge.

It's not as if I lack anything. I have good friends and a job that I enjoy. We manage financially. I have a husband and children and a wide circle of friends. Physically I keep fit. But this restlessness makes me uneasy. But quasi-psychological reasoning is only superficial. You shouldn't think too much, otherwise you only make yourself unhappy. You should seize the day and forget the big questions. What do you think as a professional?

But she did not wait for an answer.

She had spoken without interruption long after we had got off the train and she then disappeared into the crowd of people.

Beauty as a sign

Père Lachaise cemetery

I am on my way to seek out the Paris which perhaps more than many others has maintained art as solace, the search for beauty as a guide in a spiritual journey. So I am leaving the west bank of Bohemians and taking the back streets past the beautiful bisexual people in the Marais Quarter. They hang out in their pubs and pavement cafés. I cross the town and come eventually to the Cimitière du Père Lachaise – the cemetery near the boulevard de Ménilmontant. Late that afternoon I park the bicycle in a dirty parking place. It smells of petrol from the thundering traffic. Just inside the entrance it is calm.

Together with a crowd of other people I allow myself to be shoved into this enormous site. Practically all of the cultural giants seem to be buried here: musicians, artists and sculptors – those who have left behind enduring masterpieces. I am holding a small map in my hand. It is an idea to make a sort of cultural walk and quiz.

This cemetery is obviously a place of pilgrimage. A great many languages whirl around about me. People move quietly as if in devotion. Young men with shaved heads stand together with the pierced jeans wearers next to the Rock singer Jim Morrison's grave (1943–1971). Some of them sit reverently next to their lighted candles. Several write small pieces of paper which they push in under the stones next to his grave. Others stand motionless in silent devotion after laying flowers on the gravel. When I see their faces full of reverence I think of the Wailing Wall in Jerusalem. There the pious orthodox Jews bob back and forth. They also put small scraps of paper into the wall. But here in Paris it is not Yahweh or God who is honoured but one of Rock music's martyrs; one who went before in spontaneous combustion.

Frédéric Chopin (1810–1849), who lies not far from Morrison, asked to have several spadesful of genuine Polish earth on his grave. He always longed for home. When I stand near his gravestone I can hear a faint nocturne in my mind. Who does not feel reverence when they hear his études or quiet waltzes in minor keys. I see that the artist Modigliani (1884–1920) – he of the rectangular portraits of women – has his final resting place here. He also longed for home. His last words were reported to be: '*Cara Italia, Cara Italia.*' Modigliani lived at approximately the same time as Giacometti and the writer Samuel Beckett but was never acknowledged during his lifetime. Now someone has placed an enormous bouquet of yellow flowers at his grave. Modigliani has received enormous rehabilitation. Posters and reproductions of his lengthened faces hang in student corridors and on kitchen walls across the entire world.

I am looking for the family grave where the author Marcel Proust rests (1871–1922). With his meticulous language he draws out intensity from existence. He particularly tries to capture and convey an experience of beauty's timelessness. I finally find the square gravestone. Someone has placed a large bunch of roses there this morning. Next to the flowers lies a letter covered in plastic where someone with an unsteady hand has written *Merci Marcel!* The word *Merci* is underlined with two thick lines of red ink. The ink has partially dissolved through moisture and rain. I have also brought a sprig of hawthorn to lay on his grave. I bow before the intermediary of Beauty and Feelings.

Reading Proust – an inner journey

The novel *In search of lost time* (1913–1927) has been read and loved. Much the same can be said of Proust as of other giants of literature: James Joyce, Robert Musil or Fyodor Dostoevsky. They are difficult to read to the end. Many people have guilty consciences when it comes to Proust, as they have never read further than page eighty-nine in the first book, where the famous Madeleine cakes are eaten and an entire childhood world appears in front of the writer of the story. One should be suspicious of anyone who says they have read the whole suite of novels. Few have been able to finish Proust's novel, which consists of seven books amounting to some three thousand pages. Even more readers, such as myself, have given up after several volumes. It does not matter that so many of us return time and time again – deeply fascinated. Not to remember each character in the turmoil of the turn of the century bourgeoisie, or to follow the intrigue, but to bathe, or rather, relax in the author's manner of slowly unfolding sentence after sentence. The central point is not so much what happens in the book but the state that is brought about by the meandering trails of the language. To allow oneself to be carried away on the tortuous swell of words borders on meditation. Marcel Proust can be said to represent beauty's role in the inner life and art as a pathway to spiritual awareness.

Through Proust's text we read in a remarkable way about ourselves. We notice the world with a new freshness when we look up from the book. Perhaps this is because there is an *uncertainty* throughout the entire book – the position of the author changes. Proust does not work with a distinct and all-knowing narrator who looks down on his fictitious characters' lives and repeats what happens to them during a certain period of time.

Not even after reading through the enormous amount of text do we have any idea of what the author – Marcel – looks like.

Perhaps it is this fluctuating author subject which makes *In search of . . .* an 'awareness novel' – a world is unrolled before the reader's eyes. The narrator is a passive listener, an eyewitness. This means that the novel's real drama takes place within the author's/reader's own subconscious.

A time beyond time?

The title of Proust's novel is slightly misleading. On one level it can seem as if the narrator's project is to *remind* himself of memories that have disappeared, make a journey into the corridors of forgetfulness. In the oceans of human destinies in the work and interiors from the turn of the twentieth century's aristocratic lives, there is a wealth of psychological reflections on memory and remembrance. Nearly all Proust readers can remember how the main character conjured up an entire epoch of his childhood in Combray by tasting the famous cake dunked in camomile tea.

At the same time the suite of novels touches another kind

of journey. It is only partially to do with past time. Rather Proust tries to reach a world of experience where time has stood still. He identifies episodes of boundlessness which face towards immortality: '. . . until I myself seemed actually to have become the subject of my book; a church, a string quartet or the rivalry between Francois I and Charles V' (*Swann's World*).

The feeling of being absorbed into the cosmos gives rise to a feeling of the greatest happiness. The world that the narrator meets – outside the boundaries of the self – is eternal and indestructible. 'To find oneself' is outside the observable. It is just as real, but only in quickly fleeting moments. It appears sometimes when he listens to music, reads or looks at art. His search does not only apply to the time that passes but rather to that which exists *outside* time. Proust takes the reader on a journey beyond the landscape of the past.

Proust was apparently influenced by the British draughtsman and art theoretician John Ruskin. Through his observations of paintings, façades, altars and churches Ruskin stressed that beauty has an absolute value for mankind. It is therefore the artist's – or for that matter, the author's and musician's, task to remind us of the eternal, indestructible values in existence, in such a way that the reader, observer or listener takes part in them. Ruskin's thinking is woven into *In search of time past*. At the same time Proust maintains an independent attitude. The only aesthetic enjoyment remains unproductive and passive. It is rather the artistic creative act which is life-giving.

Among other things the novel deals with the idea that man must stop seeking beauty outside himself and chasing after powerful experiences. The life-gourmets, intellectual giants or art lovers finally lose only themselves in their hunt for new reading experiences or artistic expression. Swann – one of the characters in *In search of time past,* shows himself to be deadlocked into a position of observing and enjoying life. Instead, Proust appears to state that man himself must put beauty *into* life. The whole novel finishes with an acknowledgement of man as creator.

To enter into something greater – on art as spirituality

Through Proust's books many people have gained a language for those periods of timelessness which can be experienced in music and art. We can perhaps say that Proust represents a kind of internal spirituality.

He demonstrates that there are short or long periods in life when the clock stops and eternity takes over. It is pockets of time such as these, zones of overwhelming intensity that Proust sometimes describes. Beauty gives a certain balm to the troubled heart – the mellow tones which we have touched on before and which are inbuilt in life's condition. Both culture and nature contain an overtone which Proust extracts from a sentence; the sense of another reality.

Let us listen to a keen Swedish reader of Proust, Claes Hylinger:

> It is the experience that there is something more real than the world that we live in. The sense of this and the occasional manifestation of it – the episode with the Madeleine cake is only one of these occasions, when he experiences a state of happiness and security which differentiates itself from everyday life just as much as consciousness differs from sleep – recur as a leitmotiv throughout the novel, like the short phrase of Vinteuil's sonata which surges forth, subsides and returns again and again, 'stemming as if from another world'.

In some ways, Proust is a kind of platonic idealist. He seems to say that we all live in a world of shadows, but that art opens up passageways into the real world. But Proust's 'other world' is never distinctly described. Neither is it connected to a confession of faith, a church or a religion. It does not matter that the meeting with the kingdom of art is life changing for several of the novel's characters. Let us look at some short examples.

The author finds himself out in the countryside: 'I once again ask myself what this unknown state could be, which does not contain any logical proof but conveys such a tangible and blissful reality that all other realities are but pale by comparison' (*Swann's World*).

In another place the experience of reading gives the same feeling of immensity: 'One of these fragments afforded me such incomparably intense joy that I experienced somewhere deep within my soul, in a layer of my soul that was more comprehensive and more harmonious than my remaining ego and where no obstacles or restrictions were any longer thought to exist' (*Swann's World*).

The narrator experiences something similar through music:

> As soon as he heard it, the little snatch of music had the power to open up within him the space it needed, the proportions of Swann's soul were changed by it. A margin was reserved in him for bliss that also did not correspond to any external object, and yet, instead of being purely individual, like the enjoyment of that love, assumed for Swann a reality superior to that of concrete things. The little phrase awoke within him a thirst for an unfamiliar delight, but it did not give him anything precise to assuage it ... and since he had searched the little phrase for a meaning to which his understanding could not descend, what strange drunkenness he felt as he divested his innermost soul of all the help of reason and forced it to pass alone through the sieve, through the dark filter of sound.
>
> *Swann's World*

Hylinger summarizes Proust's points:

> Both true reality and a full life are always close but are hidden; we do not see them. And that which prevents us is egotism and conceit ... the truth in life, the real world, is within reach the whole time – it is we who are unreal and because of this cut off from it. We have built our own prison. It is artistic expression which opens a kind of door in to this state.

On lovability – the elderly couple in Les Halles

One day I go down to the enormous market under the Metro station, Les Halles. It is there that I notice them. A greying elderly couple looking at each other the whole time. They are completely absorbed in their conversation. They are standing in front of me in the queue to the check-out. Those waiting behind them easily become irritated when the queue stops. Disco music is blaring from the loud speakers. Slightly distracted glances from the people rushing in to buy food.

While the old couple are talking to each other they gaze deeply into each other's eyes. Both have intensive gazes. They are discussing in detail one of Mozart's string quartets, the one in G minor. The man is arguing that the cello should be more prominent in the penultimate movement. The woman rigorously shakes her head and emphasizes instead its suppressed sound. The matter is vital to her. Once again the queue stops.

They look as if they are at least eighty years old. He wears an overcoat which is dark brown. It has an aged patina, an elegance which borders on the decadent. It is well worn and torn. His yellow neckerchief is slung around his neck with an obviously conscious nonchalance. The network of veins on his nose bears witness to one or two glasses of wine. Refinement is visible in the man's white hair and thin eyebrows. The woman wears careful but discreet make-up. She wears a brooch on her blouse which is in contrast to the dark green costume; amber mounted in silver. Her bearing is slightly stooped. The whole time they are conversing intensively. They collect up their purchases without looking at the cashier. Instead they have come to the question of the difference between how Mozart depicts the key of G minor in the two symphonies: the major symphony number 40 and the minor symphony, number 25. The inner world with its artistic values is obviously more important than the toothpaste or the piece of cheese that they have bought.

When they reach the exit I notice that the man stops,

holds open the door and bows slightly to his beloved. They look tenderly at each other and the conversation stops for ten measured seconds. She also nods, no, she bows and smiles. And then they glide quietly through the glass doors out into morning Paris. In their hands they hold plastic bags. They lean towards each other and hold each other's hands tightly as they walk away into the wind and disappear down the street.

In the midst of the glaring colours of the price reduction and the half-eaten hamburgers in the rubbish bins it is there – a touch of elegance. A whiff of a rich inner life, a mild and quiet politeness, a chivalrous movement, a touch of central European refinement which has still not disappeared. In their conversation there were no marks of the culture snob's self-absorption. In their bows there was honour, respect and appreciation. And I think of how the amiable politeness seems to slowly melt away – as reminiscences from a distant epoch.

Wasn't it old Montaigne who thought that politeness, the chivalrous or courteous, costs little and gives a great deal in exchange, as to honour others gives honour in return? Amiability and honour stay firmly rooted; anyone who gives them away still retains them.

Music that opens a hidden door

Mozart's music does not merit a mention by Proust, rather he talks about his own fictional composer; Vinteuil.

Music is thought to create a clearer impression of timeless things than nature or literature. In *In search of ...* the reader hears again and again of 'the other worldly character' in the andante movement for violin and piano by Vinteuil. But the spiritual quality of music first becomes clear a long way into the novel. From being a sound in the background in the fashionable salons, the snatch of music turns into something that deeply affects him:

> At first he had only enjoyed the beauty of the sound that the instrument produced. And he had been gripped by a strong

feeling of happiness when listening to the violin's delicate, fixed, recurring and dominant melody line. But suddenly he had become captivated by something that he could neither differentiate nor put a name to. He had tried to grasp hold of the phrase or chord (he did not know which) that glided past him and opened his soul in the same way that the scent of some roses in the damp evening air has the special ability to dilate one's nasal passages. It cannot be attributed to any other type of impression. Such an impression is, for a short moment *sine materia.*

Swann's World

In a similar way to the story in Greek mythology about how the kingdom of the dead became silent when Orpheus sang, so our anxiety about the end of life diminishes when music plays. The narrator listens to music as if to 'a promise that there existed something other than the emptiness I found in all entertainments and even in love, something which could perhaps be realized in art; and if my life seems so conceited, it had at least left some things accomplished'.

The duality when face to face with the experience of music's 'reality content' remains however. At least that is how it seems when the narrator later argues:

I knew that I would never forget this new joyous sound; this call to a supernatural joy. But could it ever become reality for me? This question seems so much more important to me since this snatch of music could interpret better than anything else, the impressions that often appeared in my past life at long intervals, like objectives and foundations to build a real life on. And this is so, precisely because they are in stark contrast to the visible world and to all my other existence. Experiences such as the one before the church tower in Martinville and the tree in Balbec. This is the strangest thing I have ever felt – a joy of an unknown sort.'

The Prisoner

Yes, how shall we understand the role of beauty or art for the inner life? Just like the narrator in the novel, many search for something 'more' via culture. Proust's point seems to be that this world of experience gives vague, but nevertheless no less meaningful, indications of another non-earthly reality. But he does not express himself clearly in the question of if there *exists* an actual external spiritual reality, independent of mankind. He has a more hesitant, reserved, attitude. His various characters have different opinions.

From the perspective of the inner journey, the point is however clear – and here I connect it to Christian spirituality. It is important that people identify the worlds of beauty that they are most affected by. During such fleeting moments there is a simultaneous sadness or a melancholy – the knowledge that good things don't last. Beauty therefore activates another side of life; that which we previously called longing or a feeling of homelessness – mankind's fundamental anxiety. We come closer to a further dimension in the inner journey.

The pain of beauty – how it speaks to one's feelings

I relive a dream. That I am standing alone in a churchyard.
Everywhere heather glow
as far as the eye can reach. Who am I waiting for? A friend.
Why doesn't he come? He's here already.

and I waken to that unshakeable PERHAPS that
carries me through the wavering world.
And each abstract picture of the world is as impossible as
The blue-print of a storm.
    Tomas Tranströmer, from *The Wild Market Square* (1983)

The man who bowed

I am at a seminar one day. I go up to the main entrance to the Sorbonne. It is cold and rainy. Mist is coming down over the city. The Parisians have a peculiar method of wrapping their scarves several extra times around their necks with a studied nonchalance. Now the scarves are practically covering their heads. The shoes of the passers-by splash in the puddles. Elderly gentlemen in dark red neck scarves with dark jackets. If I squint, the street looks like a painting by Toulouse-Lautrec.

In the dim university lecture hall in the Sorbonne the delegates are waiting: Several monks from a monastery in the town – they appear to be psychoanalysts. A couple of psychiatrists who are now training to be priests and then all these researchers: specialists on the Fathers of the Church, philosophers, historians, anthropologists. The theme is art and religion. Here sit social workers, literature experts and several students. It will be a difficult day for all Francophiles – the language of the conference is English. There will be long and exhaustive lectures on mysticism and art, on spirituality and projections, on symbols and metaphors and on spirituality and psychoanalysis. Names such as Kristeva, Lacan and Freud are as frequent as Thomas Aquinas, Simone Weil or Gregory the Great. They fly above our heads.

A long internal discussion breaks out between two Dutch researchers. The question is in which meaning the term *logos* in the New Testament is a symbol which refers to something outside itself, or if the Word is bearer of that to which it refers. No-one really understands what they mean.

But the psychoanalytical friends seize their chance and embark on a somewhat difficult-to-follow exposition of Freud's symbol theory. Freud maintains that the symbols of dreams both reveal and conceal at the same time, they are quasi-visual compromise images on the borders between the stated and the unsayable, the longed for and the feared. But because of this they shield the sleepers from waking. The dreams mediate between the conscious and the unconscious – which is the reason for the fascinating force of the symbols. Symbols function as receptacles of psychic material, 'What a choice of words!' I think to myself.

The specialists of the Early Church's symbol theory are silent and seem to find it difficult to see the connection between Freud and the spiritual fathers. A woman nods in agreement and points to Gregory of Palamas's greatness in the question of negative theology. A young man joins in.

Smoking eagerly he puts forward such texts as 'the morphology of silence', a theme in mediaeval theology. He is strikingly verbose despite the character of the subject. The unexpressed possesses strength. The Catholic priests listen absent-mindedly and chew gum. Some of the students read *Le Soir* under the desks until the afternoon.

On the left of the room sits a young orthodox priest. He is practically immobile. He has a slight beard and follows the discussion eagerly. With his intense dark brown eyes he looks with attention at each person who speaks, like a spectator following the ball at a tennis match. His contributions are few, curt and knife-sharp. They act as a watershed in the discussion. But he does not argue – he merely shows the consequences of opinions already stated. He is intensively present and lively despite his taciturnity. One barely notices it but he has a slight, virtually indiscernible smile on his lips.

Just before the meeting closes I raise my eyes. High up in one of the corners of the room is a single icon. I have not seen it previously. It is brown, tasteless and dusty. The room does not seem to have been cleaned for months. One can barely distinguish Christ's face under the dirt. It hangs there unnoticed among all this intellectual preoccupation.

After several hours we collect up our briefcases and collect our notes. The group will soon have dispersed across the town. Scraping chairs, ringing laughter and happy cries before the evening's dinner. Just before I leave I look back into the room and notice that young Russian priest. The conference hall is nearly empty. The clothes that are strewn about are picked up and the caretaker has already started to clean the chalk off the board. The Russian priest is still standing completely still. His eyes are intensively directed towards the icon. He stands immobile for a long, long time in deep concentration. Then he makes the sign of the Cross followed by a deep bow.

Compunctio – holy tears

The entire company moves on to the Rue Rivoli. Today it is Indonesian food. The atmosphere is stimulating. One of the

French nuns is also a doctor – an unusual combination. When she hears that I am writing about beauty she talks about various aspects of sorrow and pain. She says that everyone agrees that pain has a physiological as well as a psychological side. Research has shown a great deal about pain receptors. All palliative medicine is full of attempts to alleviate suffering. But she explains that the Father of the Church, Gregory (540–604) states that there is another type of pain – the bitter-sweet pain on the borders of joy and sorrow. It is that which overwhelms man in the middle of a poignant moment of beauty. People are sometimes moved when they are present at a concert. They get a lump in their throats and a shiver runs up their spines when they listen to music by Scarlatti or Arvo Pärt. Where do these tears come from?

Well, she says:

> This combination of harmony and melancholy which can be found in the absolutely finest moments can of course be interpreted as sentimentality. But another way of understanding them is as perceptions, passing hints of another eternal world. This aesthetic theology has been developed by some of the Fathers of the Church. Gregory the great spoke of *compunctio* – holy anguish. The sorrow which some feel when confronted with the most beautiful is at the same time a reminiscence of and a foretaste of the divine world. It gives a perception that God *is*, but not *who* He is.
>
> The experience of art is therefore not a subjective quality of feeling but an expression of an objective proposition. The feelings that come over a person open gateways into something Other. Here, Gregory goes a step further than Proust's 'perhaps'.
>
> Originally *compunctio* was a medical term which signified an intense physical pain, but when Gregory used the word he spoke of a psychic or spiritual torment. Gregory was called 'the doctor of longing' because of his teaching about the soul's longing for God. The bitter-sweet experience affects man's homelessness in an incomplete world, his simultaneous memory of, and longing for completeness. This spiritual lack becomes painfully tangible when faced with beauty.

Perception as the memory of something lost

According to the study of *compunctio* the pain is caused because man – outside the Paradise of Eden – experiences that something has been lost, but does not know exactly what. As a consequence of this, the whole of life is played out against a feeling of latent sorrow. The cause of the tears is that man, through his perceptions is reminded of his pilgrim status – he is on a journey. He lives in exile but is on a journey to his ultimate homeland. The melancholy of music is therefore God's dealings with man, through which he awakens man to consciousness of his origin.

According to the mediaeval theologians, the idea of pain was to remind man of his origins, to perceive his longing for eternity. In the midst of the lost and the longed for, the holy tears well up.

The sounds of the organ – on longing as hunger

There has been too much talk. I become both moved and confused. For a long time I have sought an opportunity to hear Widor's fifth organ concert. One evening I take myself off to the church of Saint Sulpice. Here there is a gigantic organ. People come into the cathedral. Bags are placed on the pews. Most have their outdoor clothes on. Outside can be heard the noise of the traffic. Inside silence reigns. So it starts. The first movement is nearly unbearably majestic. Then the last movement sounds, *toccata allegro* heavenly in its love of dancing rhythm.

But I can't help thinking of what the nun had said. That we get a lump in our throats, as now during an organ concert, or when we gasp in admiration when our children sing (out of tune) in a choir, is not only a consequence of the fact that we are simply moved, but is an indication of eternity, that it addresses us but is difficult to digest. But to paraphrase Sidner's words in the *Christmas Oratorio*:

> One concept that has always fascinated me is Divine Inspiration. To divinely *inspire* someone. There is an activity in the word that makes one believe that the subject is the one

who anticipates whilst my firm conviction … is that *we are reached by* Divine Inspiration. The source of Divine Inspiration is outside us. It is the beacon in the darkness. It is the beam of light that sweeps around the vault of heaven, time after time, and searches and now and then, it happens that a scrap of its light brushes against us and reaches into the deepest strata of our consciousness. I would like to say: I was divinely inspired.

Longing as a form of address

… The world – a labyrinth of objects mislaid and forgotten
  from the ancient swords
in the never opened graves of the Bronze Age

to the bifocals that vanished yesterday,
– it retains them all. No cause for alarm.

And you, going around in search so ardently,
Might you be an object someone is looking for?

And it occurs to you, one night when a thing
Turns up again, scratched and rusty, but the same

in a box awash with bolts and padlocks
that all this looking for objects

did no more than mirror your own craving:
that someone just as ardently might look for you.

Lars Gustafsson, from 'Elegy on objects mislaid and forgotten',
Preparation for the winter season (1990)

An American in Paris

There is something paradoxical about the whole affair. One evening I am sitting in the middle of a colourful and lively Paris, talking to an elderly American priest. He has lived here for several years. He has a broad American accent. He is gruff and friendly. His eyes are bright. Often he seems to look straight past me. His face is lined and tired-looking but he suddenly laughs with gusto. He is wearing a T-shirt with braces. We discuss the book that I am trying to write, about the disappearance of pilgrims and on culture as a solace. It appears that he himself has made a long journey through life. He started as a researcher in neurochemistry but could not escape from his interest in art. He worked in his spare time for several years as an art gallery owner in New York Then his life reached a crisis. Neither science nor art could slake his inner thirst.

After coming across Abbé Pierre's Emmaus movement, where he discovered the paradoxical riches of poverty – that it is better to give than to receive – he entered a Catholic order. He now lives on the bread line, in order to help those whose lives are even more difficult. He is well acquainted with Paris's underworld. Now and then he nods to one of the rough sleepers who pass on the hunt for beer cans. He is vociferous in his criticism of France's Welfare System. His grey hair stands on end, his hands are broad and his hand-shake is strong. Next to him on the park bench is a greasy Pizza Hut carton, next to that a well-used Bible.

Seldom have I met someone so outspoken. He is not shy of voicing his opinions. He never avoids controversial subjects. At the same time, he listens intently and seriously. A great sense of humour and resounding laughter are occa-sionally replaced by a steady stare which looks right through me without blinking. When he talks he does so from an inner core of strength. He is not embarrassed to state that his starting point is an unwavering faith, some-thing that most people shy away from.

The melancholy of life's journey

When he hears my argument about beauty as a breath of holiness he looks completely bewildered. Although he is a great lover of culture – he follows jazz concerts, art exhibi-tions as well as the sports results – he seems to have taken one step *beyond* the consolation of culture. He is quietly enthusi-astic when he wants to describe his Christian interpretation of both beauty and melancholy. Squinting, he looks out over Paris's garish street life, lights his pipe and explains.

His reasoning is clear: there is one aspect of the human condition that people can never escape from, but must confront; the instinct that life is fundamentally tragic. Happiness or the joy of life must of course be celebrated, but people must also have the courage to approach the glaring revelation that wonderful things never last, that even the beauty of culture is fleeting, and that the whole of life is just transitory.

He thinks that our life cycle contains an in-built sorrow. People can ignore this feeling for long periods at a time, living instead for their future, their children, their work, their friends or even their studies or for constant new and interesting cultural excursions which are interesting in themselves. 'All this has value – more quality of life, more laid-back attitudes and less chasing the wind! We need more people who just chill out and take it easy ' he says and laughs. But now and then even those who enjoy life are gripped by a vague panic and ask, 'Is this really all there is?' These occasional periods of anxiety should not be ignored.

This longing for 'something more' is especially relevant as life constricts with approaching middle age, after a divorce or when illness strikes. It could be that their love lives are in crisis, a child grows up and leaves home, a loved one dies or suffers needlessly, the terrors of war are unbearably close or they see their own bodies ageing or changing. When life's difficulties become more apparent they are reminded of a more deep-seated loneliness. 'Then it doesn't help to play golf or to travel to Provence to drink wine.'

The old priest starts to talk about how the entire human race has the fundamental feeling of being lost. A sort of constant homesickness stretching back to Adam and Eve and their expulsion from Paradise. 'Depths call unto depths' (Ps 42:7). And it is precisely beauty that activates this nostalgia.

People can live for long periods feeling secure and that everything is going well. But sooner or later some internal or external event takes place that tears this security apart. The alienation becomes tangible. And this developmental leap in the life cycle gives their anxieties spiritual overtones.

'Yes, yes,' I reply. 'This is well known but how can the whole thing be explained?' It is then that he says,

> This seemingly *subjective* experience of rootlessness has an *objective* basis. The anxiety comes from the heart – where God himself has placed eternity in our breasts. But because we find ourselves outside Paradise we can only feel it as 'You are in need of me'. What manifests itself as a mid-life crisis from a psychological point of view is in fact the expression of our fundamental homelessness without God.

'Gracious!' I think to myself after this perspicacious observation. This is not exactly some impartial matter-of-fact attitude. This man is not being tossed hither and thither without a compass or some aim in life. He has a purpose to his life, a centre – he is completely politically incorrect. He is a long way from postmodernity.

He continues undaunted:

> The anxiety that comes with life's crises cannot be reduced to sentimentality or regressive tendencies. It is a real feeling, just as tangible as the longing for one's lover or children – who have gone away for a while – is a witness to the fact that they actually exist. The longing is a sign that the other exists. It is the same thing here. The longing is a consequence of man's search for meaning, his ontological thirst. Outside Eden man has become disorientated. Therefore, that which from a human perspective seems in the beginning to be a general state of melancholy or fear of death and from a normal point of view can be interpreted as 'a search for meaning', is in fact God's own action on the human heart.

He explains everything slowly, but without any doubt of the importance of what he is saying.

The feeling that something is lacking

He says that he deliberately chooses to use terms such as 'spiritual homelessness' or 'thirst for spiritual rest' instead of 'the philosophical consequences of postmodernity's individualism' 'Bullshit' he says and continues:

> You must start from an ontology, an understanding of
> reality, something that is not a consequence of social
> constructions or agreements. For me this ties in with my
> experience that the Christian faith is not only useful or 'an
> answer to the meaning of life' but also *true* – this very old
> fashioned word.

Without batting an eyelid he represents through his attitude
a world of steadfastness where there is an unbiased acceptance of biblical and religious truths. Because he takes this
position, the talk of anxiety of heart is transformed into
something else: a sign, a language game.

He states that the restlessness has as its basic foundation
the fact that humans are rooted in 'another state'. The
answers given by sociologists and psychologists to the questions of confusion and longing to be 'away' are therefore
not incorrect but insufficient. Mankind in fact longs for
something 'more'. But this 'more' does not require external
movement, journeys to foreign countries, greater or more
powerful experiences, or visits to places of culture. The
journey can certainly start with the feeling that nature, art
and music border on 'Something else'. But sooner or later it
continues in a feeling that *this too* is also insufficient. In
beauty itself there is an emptiness. I start to think of Nils
Ferlin's words: 'But the most beautiful day that summer
gave meant that I longed to be there.'

Without beating about the bush, he maintains that the
rootlessness that people experience is caused because they
have torn themselves loose from a spiritual plane. The hunt
for great experiences, the feeling of existential emptiness,
and the permanent emphasis on the unique has a spiritual
driving force.

It starts to get late and we move indoors. We are sitting
in the stairwell of a semi-deserted library. Students with
torn tennis shoes, long cardigans and large earphones on
their ears wander in and out through the large door to the
reading room. Many are carrying coffee cups. Others are

standing outside the door smoking. Snatches of laughter.
The priest continues:

> Of course, you researchers will continue to look for the
> social and economic roots of a sense of not belonging. You
> should all try to understand the psychological prerequisites
> and expressions of flight/inconstancy. Of course some
> anxiety stems from childhood experiences, and there are
> certainly some causes of dissatisfaction that are connected
> to cultural divergence. But rootlessness is not *only* the
> consequence of a spinning moral compass. It really means
> that [and here he pauses before he continues] a factual tran-
> scendent world wishes to remind us of its existence.

But the ability to learn how to listen for it has practically
disappeared. There are innumerable travel agencies that can
guide people around the world – the outward journey.
There are therapists who try to help people to understand
their psychiatric development or their inner sorrows and
disappointments. But even the spiritual inner journey has its
basis.

Where do the existential questions come from?
Continuing, he says with dismay that the churches often
hinder themselves by presenting their own message as banal.
If the Christian faith is reduced to trivial talk about transitory feelings it is no wonder that many people opt out.
Similarly, if the churches maintain a fundamentalist view of
such things that ought to be understood purely symbolically,
it is not strange that others hesitate. If people are expected to
believe that God is like some old man with a beard sitting on
a cloud or that heaven is a place just as accessible as Paris or
Marseille, then there is little wonder that thinking people
with any honesty shy away from such belief. Without
symbols and images one cannot think about religion.

'Yes, but tell me about this homeless stage,' I say. He fills
his pipe and looks out of the window. Some children are
swinging on broken swings whilst the parents stand under a
tree smoking. An ambulance goes past in the street outside.

Well, I have found – and this is, incidentally, in keeping with all the great mystical traditions from John of the Cross to Simone Weil – that the most important 'step' that God takes when He wishes to draw someone back to Himself is that he lets them face a fundamental confusion within themselves. God reminds the person that He exists by allowing them to be anxious because they cannot find any stability in their existence. And the fact that people *are* aware of the metaphysical basis of homelessness is God's own way of communicating with their inner being.

He screws up his eyes a little when he asks me to take note of the topsy-turvy way of thinking and then says in an even more provocative way: 'This fundamental anxiety is the work of The Other, not a manifestation of psychiatric problems.'

Obviously this man – well schooled in evolution theory and modern scientific theory – has a well-integrated theocentric understanding of reality. He states that the original cause and ultimate goal of existence and mankind centres around God – as he made himself known in the man in the icon. God, not mankind, is the hub of existence. But, he says, this method of reasoning has practically disappeared from the agenda. It is considered strange, intellectually inferior or threateningly deviant. Nevertheless this is how the Christian tradition thought right from the beginning.

He continues:

The insight into the *spiritual* cause of rootlessness is the decisive point in the inner journey. But it presupposes that one has the courage to question the most frequent fallacy of our age: that the material or social existence is everything. Most people start to think when they are sad or depressed that they must search for the cause of this in the various crises of childhood, the traumas of growing up or the stressful conditions of their working lives. All these factors are important – I find this especially when I work with refugees or addicts. But woven into the emptiness I also come across another dimension. This is a threatening statement for the person who has been used to thinking that everything stems from them.

Do you think I'm kidding, man?
We decide to meet again several days later. He comes from a funeral. He works out in Drancy. AIDS is constantly harvesting its victims, he says. Tired, he rests his head in his hands and looks out at the taxis rushing past. The constant noise of traffic, men with their hands in their pockets, girls in school uniforms and women with mobile telephones assails our ears. What he now says sounds even more radical.

'Right,' he says, 'this emptiness which is found like a side effect of both beauty and longing, paradoxically contains a *hint of* that which people are lacking.' His eyes light up when he quotes St Augustine: 'You shall not seek me if you have not already found me' and 'Consider Lord, that my thirst for You is Your own work'.

He explains that he usually advises those who feel anxiety to consider that it is an expression of an objective reality. 'A person who has feelings of longing must – either alone or together with a friend or spiritual advisor – identify when, how and in which context they are conscious of these overtones in both beauty and rootlessness.'

I usually say: 'When you start to perceive the depths in your own rootlessness – remind yourself that this is not imagination. Somebody wants something for you by making you feel emptiness. And thus begins the wandering along the way that leads from a vague feeling to stability.'

We leave the library. Nike and Dolce Gabbana advertisements are highly illuminated in the middle of the austere turn of the century architecture. A little way off a group of teenagers are playing basket ball. The sweaty T-shirts are very bright and they are shouting excitedly to each other. You can hear the thuds against the asphalt; some are sitting out next to a garage entrance, drinking Sprite. A late afternoon in chilly Paris – a prayer from a priest from a distant epoch.

He empties his pipe and looks at his watch. He has an appointment. He is on his way to yet another funeral. Before he goes he says in his strong southern drawl: '*Do you think I'm kidding, man?*' It is obvious that I mean that another world exists and that we have the memory of it somewhere deep within us. The secret of it is that it has been made manifest to us in what we call the Incarnation – but we'll have to discuss that another time. '*You're a scholar*', he says, 'and you are perhaps thinking of Plato or some other idealism. Do that of course, theories are interesting. But I prefer to take the risk – to believe that the longing is a code from The Other. Didn't you say that you have an icon in your pocket? Do you really think that your longing is just an evolutionary remnant or a regressive desire? *Brother, it ain't necessarily so.*'

Chapter Eight

VENICE IN THE WINTER RAIN – ON THE ICON'S GAZE IN THE DARKNESS

The black image
Framed in silver worn to
   shreds by kisses ,
The black image framed in
   silver
Worn to shreds by kisses
Framed in silver
The black image worn to
   shreds by kisses
Framed in silver
The black image worn to
   shreds by kisses
All round the image
The white silver worn to
   shreds by kisses
All round the image
The very metal worn to
   shreds by kisses
Framed in metal
The black image worn to
   shreds by kisses

The Darkness, O, the darkness
Worn to shreds by kisses
The Darkness in our eyes
Worn to shreds by kisses
All we wished for
Worn to shreds by kisses
All we never wished for
Kissed and worn to shreds by
   kisses
All we escaped
Worn to shreds by kisses
All we wish for
Kissed and kissed again.

Gunnar Ekelöf, 'Diwan over the Prince of Emgion'

Bellissimo!

Today I am passing over the Alps and through the Brenner Pass. A chill hangs over the dark motorways as I thunder south. A little while ago I passed Innsbruck, took myself up onto Europabrücke and further through a number of tunnels. Like a giant necklace lowered from the sky, the

A22 motorway hangs elegantly over the steep massif. Articulated lorries drive dangerously close to one another as they
toil up tough slopes or brake in long downward inclines.
White Alfa Romeos rush past as fast as lightening down
towards the Italian Po valley. My little car dashes along and
I spot the exit signs: Trento and Bolzano. A little while later
I turn off the autostrada, pay the toll and drive down
towards the west. Hilly alpine landscape. Serpentine roads
up into the mountains. It gets dark. Late at night I find
a hotel on a hillside. I ring the bell for a long time before a
ten-year-old comes and opens the door. He is holding
a computer game in one hand and a bunch of keys in the
other. World-weary he shows me around and gives me the
room key. He takes my name from my passport and writes
it down in a sprawling hand. In the night I hear the rain on
the roof.

Sunday morning. Translucent clear air in the December
sun. The shadows are long. The church bells have a broken
ring as they ring out over the blue-black Idros lake. The
lake lies like a mirror after yesterday's downpour. Ducks
with their heads tucked under their wings bob up and down
on the waves a little way out in the bay. They are barely
visible from the beach. I am several miles west of Lake
Garda.

Suddenly something happens. A veteran car rally passes
through the village. Shining cars from the 1930s and 40s.
Bright colours. Dark green leather seats. Swarthy men sit in
the drivers' seats next to their well-dressed ladies, looking
in the rear-view mirrors. The women wear pastel dresses
and earrings – plastic shells; a former fashion. The deafening din of the engines is replaced after several hectic minutes
by the grey-green peace of December. The quiet splendour
of flowers. The clearness of the air is just as restful as late
autumn's remaining scent. It runs like balsam down into the
valleys.

It is seductively beautiful. The greenery billows up over
the walls of the houses. Lowing cows are standing a little
way up on a hillside. Cypresses sway in the wind. Elderly

men look with squinting eyes next to the roadside. Grand-
mothers sit on park benches in conversation whilst watching their grandchildren. A mother gives her four-year-old
lad yesterday's stale bread. Together they feed the ducks.
Here on the southern side of the lake it appears sunken like
a Norwegian fjord.

From time to time tourists stop near the terrace where I
am sitting. Hot passengers climb out of crowded cars and
stand dumbfounded in wonder. 'Fantastic! What a view.
Enchanting.' '*Schön. Siehst du Ulrich, was?*' The expressions are different but the mutual opinion is enchantment:
'*Great ! Marvellous!*' exclaim some American women. The
Italians agree and nod: '*Bellissimo*'. Before the company
moves further on they remain standing by their car doors.
They can hardly bear to take their eyes off the view. I buy
myself a small postcard to keep in my office. The card can
never capture the majestic space over the lake, its quiet
power, but it is loaded with the strength of the experience.
What was it the tourist researchers called it? Oh yes, the
evocative power of souvenirs.

The buses leave, the dust settles and the view to the north
once again becomes visible – and the birdsong returns.
Nature's muted sounds are often suppressed by the noise of
civilization. As I listen, I think of Tomas Tranströmer's
short haiku poem: 'The scent of God – in the tunnel of birdsong a locked door opens.'

I drive south in the afternoon. The silhouettes of the
mountain tops stand out in relief against the grey blue mist.
Small villages are dotted along the mountain roads. Here
and there mediaeval castles. Small three-wheeled scooters
drag their burdens of hay up the nearly vertical village
roads. Old women clad in black walk across the fields, with
shambling gait.

Inside the car a calming hum starts up. It is the sound of
the air-conditioning. The traffic is still light and the engine
purrs. Imperceptibly, a vehicle is transformed into a
forward-rushing meditation room; the coupé's limited
space, quiet music and magnificent views.

Milano-Venezia A4 is the name of the thundering motorway which leads me the final 150 kilometres eastwards
towards the city of lagoons, surrounded by myths. This is
hardly meditative driving. The traffic is heavy and intense.
The six-lane autostrada rolls through the flat landscape.
Everywhere large industrial areas. Enormous tasteless advertising boards hang over the carriageway. Gigantic articulated
lorries travel in caravan. Dangerous overtaking by hot-
tempered Japanese drivers in their cars. Mercedes with tinted
windscreens glide past. I take a short break at an *autogrill*.
Red- eyed drivers lean against the bar drinking glasses of
white wine, smoking cigarettes and reading the newspapers.

An hour later I park the car in one of the back streets in
Mestre, the dormitory town on the outskirts of Venice. I
arrive late. During the afternoon the clear daylight has
turned into heavy mist. But now it is dark and rainy. I
finally find a fairly good hotel. About eleven at night the
sound of cars can no longer be heard in the streets. CNN
flickers imperceptibly on the TV. The sound does not work.
Only a few kilometres from my room are canals, gondolas,
San Marco and Caffè Florian.

Venice in the late winter gloom

It is early one winter morning in Northern Italy. Once again
the dark black coffee, tepid milk and tough bread. Several
sticky packages of marmalade and butter have been left on
the breakfast table. I leave the hotel and negotiate a dangerous crossroads to the railway station in Mestre. So the train
leaves for Venice. It rolls quickly along a thin strip of land.
We are there after only ten minutes. No-one has bothered
about my carefully bought ticket. A light rain is falling as I
exit onto the open square outside the station. In my bag is
my small computer.

Directly outside the station are the stops for the ferries –
vaporetti – Venice's water-borne bus system. The rain eases
off and a chill creeps in. I manage to find a seat right at the
front in Vaporetto number one – it goes right out to Lido,

the fashionable island which lies just outside Venice. With my hood up and my scarf wrapped round my face I sit on the first bench. The town streams past me on both sides. I soon catch a glimpse of the Rialto Bridge and the Accademia. There is a smell of diesel and the sea. Above me the high winter sky. In front of me this constantly shifting architecture – everything is mirrored in the water. The sound of the vaporetto's own roaring engine diminishes when it has picked up speed. Then the wind can be heard as well as the lapping of the dirty water against the stern post.

I travel along La Volta – the curve – it is nearly three and a half kilometres long and passes through Venice like a reversed 'S'. Officially it is called Canal Grande, but the Venetians call it *canalazzo*. It is both the artery, traffic route and promenade thoroughfare. Once upon a time trading vessels journeyed right up to the Rialto Bridge to unload their cargoes. Businessmen built palaces on both sides of the enormous canal. Now the palaces lie as ornaments, each one chiselled out in stone. The architecture is deafening, the mirroring of the façades in the water is magnificent.

It is of course a confused city, with a row of canals, bridges, small parks and piazzas. On the canals a seemingly endless variety of large vessels, taxi boats, gondolas, garbage boats, ferries, luxury cruisers and ambulance boats dart around. Here and there are barges fully laden with timber, food and beer crates. Sometimes the roar of the boat engines is insistent, but even more important is the wind. Flags flap in the blast. I hear the sound of ropes jerking at the buoys. The poles to which the bobbing gondolas are moored are red and white striped like peppermint rock. Nowhere are there accelerating Mercedes or howling Hyundai. Silence and the severe chill in the air are balm after a couple of days' rushing along Europe's motorways.

It has been said that there is still no overall map of this city of lagoons. But this rumour very likely belongs to the tourist industry's stereotypical idea of Venice: the myth of the magic city. But the rumour is true; Venice is the best city on earth to get lost in. If one gets tired then the nearest vaporetto is only a few minutes away. From there one can always ask the way. If nothing else one can go back to the railway station, Ferrovia.

It is therefore sometimes necessary to hop off the vaporetto – even if it can feel unsafe – to wander along the small alleyways, to follow a strip of light which leads down into the quarter and can suddenly dazzle the observer in the middle of a glistening canal. Gondoliers break out into 'O Sole Mio' with rusty voices. Sometimes one notices an open window. One catches a whiff of cooking food. A figure pops up in the darkness and then disappears again. Small streets suddenly open up into a peaceful square in front of an old palace.

Venice did not get its name until the thirteenth century. I read that an important date in the city's history is 828. It was then that the relics of St Mark were transported here from Alexandria in Egypt (yes, in actual fact it was a daring theft). Immediately the inhabitants began to build a church in his memory. The building started just as someone found a convenient legend about him. When Mark had carried out his missionary work an angel appeared to him in a dream. The angel said that this very marshy ground was where he should be buried and be made a saint. The apparition of the angel and the lion – the symbol of the evangelist Mark, can be seen in the nearly four-metre-long painting in the Palazzo Ducale painted by Vittorio Carpaccio in 1516. Since then the lion has also been a symbol of the city of Venice.

The mosaic in the cathedral ceiling

The icon's steady gaze

Venice in winter is slightly less chaotic than during the summer. When I disembark from the vaporetto at the Piazza San Marco I am certainly not alone, but the square is not packed with tourists – a rarity in this famous city. Of course, pigeons swarm around me. I pass the Caffè Florian on my left, glance up towards the campanile and place myself in the middle of Venice's only large square. In front of me is Saint Mark's – the Cathedral. With its cupolas and spires, multi-coloured marble columns, shimmering gold mosaics, arches crowned by creamy-white plant ornamentation that at one time was gilded, and masses of sculptures, it is like a massive gateau or an oriental jewel chest. The gold glistens in the pale winter light.

I look up at the church's façade. The mosaics still have their original colours from the thirteenth century and are stunning in their brilliance. The north portal tells of the translation of St Mark's relics from Alexandria to Venice.

The interior of the cathedral is formed like any Byzantine or Orthodox church. The floor, covered with an unending variation of mosaics, seems to go in waves, a series of innumerable floods. I place myself right in front of the altar. Directly above the east apse I notice the icon which is similar to my little travel icon. I take out my binoculars – an invaluable item when studying the fronts of buildings. Yes, the man in the image is holding up his hand in benediction. But he has not bent his fingers so that the ring finger meets the thumb as in so many other icons.

He makes a circle with his two fingers – an ancient symbol of eternity. Another way of interpreting the two fingers of the hand raised in benediction is that they represent Christ's two natures. The three fingers which are pointing upwards are said to be a metaphor for the Trinity. The man holds a book in his hand and he looks straight down on us. Around his head is a golden halo and on it is written *ho on* (Greek for 'he who is').

Sometimes this icon is called *Christos Pantocrator, Ruler of All*. But the mosaic in this church has not got the slightest trace of quiet tranquillity. It is coarsely chiselled, brutal and exact. If I turn round and look directly to the west, there is another depiction of Christ. This is milder – more like icons in Russia, in Greek chapels or my own icon in my pocket.

I squint in the light as I come out into the wet piazza, thinking of Tomas Tranströmer's poem 'Romanesque Arches'.

Inside the huge Romanesque church the tourists jostled in
   the half darkness
Vault gaped behind vault, no complete view.
A few candle-flames flickered.
An angel with no face embraced me
and whispered through my whole body:
'Don't be ashamed of being human, be proud!
Inside you vault opens behind vault endlessly.
You will never be complete, that's how it's meant to be.'
Blind with tears
I was pushed out on the sun-seething piazza
together with Mr and Mrs Jones, Mr Tanaka and Signora
   Sabatini
and inside them all vault opened behind vault endlessly.

I converse for a moment with 'Mr and Mrs Jones, Herr
Tanaka and Signora Sabatini'. But after a while I return to
the church and go into the Choir on the right. There is
another icon, *Madonna Nicopeia* from the eleventh
century. Mary is holding the child in her arms. She squints
a little and does not look straight ahead. The icon is only
half a metre in size and is not raised up over the mass of
people, but mounted in the altar. In front of the altar stands
a woman in a queue waiting to go forward. Finally her turn
comes. She bows, falls to her knees, tenderly holds the icon
and then stands for a long time looking into its eyes.

The eyes of the icon
Afterwards I sit for a while at a café table in the giant
piazza. The gas heater hisses but I wrap myself in one of the
blankets that are available for guests and look up towards
the mosaics.

Before my eyes is demonstrated a decidedly visual and
aesthetic side of Christianity. In the Protestant world Christianity is sometimes reduced to a question of belief; or
agreeing with statements which struggle against knowledge
and proved experience – thought of by many as humbug.
This one-sided emphasis on *doctrine* has resulted in the
rejection of those particular dimensions in the world of reli-

gion which do not have anything to do with truth. And I think to myself: that religions do of course have a dogmatic side – a religious person does not just have some vague general belief , but they believe in *Something or Someone*. But a one-sided rationalistic understanding of religion means that any vague encounters with the mystical side of religion and a person's faith in the ineffable, have sometimes been rejected as intellectual deterioration.

But the way that art can conjure up a meeting with the divine, by architecture and painting as well as the obeisances and other bodily movements and gestures in the liturgy have probably a much greater meaning for a religious attitude to life than doctrine. A narrow intellectual view of religion has meant that many so-called secular people in Northern Europe feel homeless. They are fascinated by holiness but are frightened by dogma. They are attracted by the divine but mistrust its professional interpreters. They are intellectual but not emotional atheists. But to be present in holy places, to gaze on the faces of the saints, prophets and apostles or to bow down in front of them is – psychologically speaking – just as important for creating and maintaining faith as dedicating oneself to sacred texts. It is in the interplay with great stories and creativity that the religious belief gets its nourishment. The aesthetic aspect and ritual places of religion are not just insignificant by-products but a necessary prerequisite for religious experience. This is particularly true in relation to icons.

Icons are not symbolic or quasi-art. Instead, the icon is performative; it creates something. It is a manifestation of a belief, an illustration of the basic paradox itself, that existence in fact *has* a centre and this centre aims its compassionate eyes towards humankind. Pictures and materials mean just as much as abstract words and imagined ideas.

Christ is often the main figure in an icon. On many occasions he is portrayed in a bearded surrealism. At other times he is sitting as a child on his mother Mary's lap. But the icon's principal starting point is that it is the historical man

Jesus who is to be portrayed. No-one who is represented in an icon may be anonymous. But according to icon theologians, every attempt to dematerialize or spiritualize them is to deny Christianity's historical anchoring.

The Liturgy in the Eastern Church emphasizes not so much listening as seeing. Of course St Mark's Cathedral in front of me has been a Catholic church for centuries. Pious people look right through the icon direct into the image (*eikon*) of the divine which is of course Christ himself. This is not worship of graven images in the Old Testament sense – which of course lies behind its prohibition of images. Rather it is respect for God's own way of making himself known, incarnate in the world in a special person from Nazareth.

The Hellenistic culture was extremely fond of pictures. They allowed depictions of the whole pantheon of gods. This was in contrast to the Jewish prohibition of pictures where it was clearly laid down that no-one was allowed to make permanent representations of the divine. It is in this divided attitude to the religious role of images that Christianity developed.

When Christianity spread during the first centuries in the Hellenistic and Roman worlds it was made up of a mixture of Oriental and Greek culture. The Christian faith had to be made comprehensible in another context than the one in which it had started – the Jewish culture. It is in this context that one can understand the icon whether it is a mosaic on the wall as here in Saint Mark's or in Rome's San Clemente, a piece of plastic which is placed in my pocket or a piece of painted wood which is usual in the Greek or Russian country churches. Behind this devotional picture stretches a long history.

Devotional images seem to have been symbolic in the earliest Christian era – not least because of their followers' fear of persecution. The image of Jesus was portrayed as a fish, bread and wine or as a shepherd. The icon's austere image of a man who looks straight out towards the observer first appeared between AD 300–600. These images were decorated and carried around in procession. But in AD 730 icons were forbidden in the entire Byzantine world. Wall paintings were whitewashed over and replaced by simple crosses. Lovers of icons, *iconodules,* were persecuted, arrested or executed, whilst the *iconoclasts,* those who maintained that the use of icons was heathen, gained power for a short period. It wasn't until about 100 years later in AD 843, that the iconodules were triumphant through the patronage of a woman – the Empress Theodora – who ruled in her own right as widow of the icon-hating Emperor Theophilus. Theodora is actually depicted in one of the largest mosaics in Ravenna, several miles south of Venice. For the defenders of icons – who maintained that it was important to depict Christ – it was a question of safeguarding the belief that God's son had become a true man in Jesus of Nazareth. This conviction had to be fought for against the Greek philosophers – for whom the thought was offensive – but also against the Jewish belief that it was forbidden to make an image of God one could not even mention his name.

This means that the icon, the image of Christ, of Mary, underlines the paradox or madness in the Christian understanding of reality. God became man in Christ and could be seen and described. This became a constantly recurring and important argument for using icons.

The iconoclasts maintained that the reverence for icons was the same as idolatry. Those who kissed the icons, carried them in procession, or expected miracles from them were ridiculed. This was exactly how the heathens treated their idols. They further maintained that it was impossible to make oneself an image of God, whom no-one had seen. It was of course written in the second book of Moses. 'You shall not make for yourself any idol or image, whether it is of anything in Heaven, or on earth or in the waters under the earth.'

But the iconodules' argument was clear. The prohibition of pictorial representation would have to come to an end because God had become physically manifest in a historical person. And because the New Testament – the new covenant which is made between God and man – has now fulfilled the Old Testament, the point is that people have in fact seen God in the person of Jesus and can therefore portray him. If anyone denies the right of the icons then they deny God's own incarnation.

The icon is therefore not only one way of reaching contact with the divine in meditation by looking into its eyes. It is furthermore the door through which the divine reaches man.

The prototype and the spiritual energy are therefore present in the icon. This means that when someone approaches an icon – the complete depiction of God – then they, at the same time come closer to being the sort of person that they are intended to be, they are nearer their original source. The picture represents something that was, is, and is to come.

It creates a mysterious presence in the eyes of the observer, a presence which reaches into eternity. In its eyes is hidden the prodigal son's father waiting at home on the farm and looking out for the one person who, in the midst of the party's tedium 'came to his senses' and wished to return home.

The nucleus of identity – our relationship to the Other

I look around the cold square where tourists are trying to avoid flocks of pigeons and hawkers. Where I am sitting a hive of warmth builds up, partly because I am drinking *vino caldo* and partly because I am sitting near a gas heater. I take my own icon out of my pocket. I place it on the table. The most extraordinary thing about the icon is its reverse perspective. That is to say, the parallel lines do not meet at a point in the horizontal *behind* the image – something which westerners have become used to ever since the central perspective of the Renaissance – but rather at a point *in front of* the image. The iconographer perhaps wishes to emphasize the fact that he is depicting a world *beyond* the material or the earthly. A more psychological interpretation could be that the observer becomes *drawn into* the picture; the feeling of being present is strengthened by the reverse perspective. Furthermore, the light in the icon does not come from any special place in the actual motif, but from the background, which is gilded.

Nearly all figures in icons are turned towards the observer – even if the composition itself demanded another position. The saints become the contacts between man and the inscrutable. The significance of eye contact in the Byzantine mosaics is obvious. Many of them look like old-fashioned group photos. In Byzantium's piety there is however a theology of the eye, one *looks* into the kingdom of heaven. At the same time one is *seen* as a human being, observed, preserved in a glance. This reciprocity between humans and God, constitutes in its turn the nucleus of identity.

And I call to mind the words:'Now we see through a glass darkly, but then we will see face to face' (First letter of St Paul to the Corinthians 13:12).

'Look Daddy!' – *on the need to be noticed*
I put my books away and ponder over how these learned expositions could be related to a highly trivial and ordinary life. But for a while it is necessary to break away from this high-minded style. We will move to an ordinary kitchen on one ordinary morning!

All parents will recognize this: 'Look Daddy, look Daddy, look Daddy!' And the parent listlessly turns around and looks for the twenty-eighth time at the little mite who is doing a somersault on the carpet, balancing on the edge of the sofa or has just learned to juggle with two balls. It is as if a work of art cannot really be counted if we do not look at our offspring and say: 'well done', 'you are clever' or 'cool'. Children come home with masses of drawings and want us to look at them, and of course we do. But after a quick glance we look at the newspaper again. These taped-up painted toilet rolls which are meant to represent a troll, we ignore. The things that the children have made with such careful effort at nursery end up in the loft after several hours or in the back of a wardrobe. If they are lucky they are placed next to Mum's computer at the office or stuck on the fridge.

The dilemma for many children is that deep down nobody really takes any notice of them. Deep down it is a matter of a basic need – just as strong as the need for water, food or sleep – to be seen, acknowledged – to be taken seriously. This need remains throughout our lives. It's as if we do not really exist if no-one sees us.

So the years pass. And the need for another type of acknowledgment grows. It is much deeper than that of friends, the family or work colleagues. We sense an inner aching loneliness, not least when the children have grown up, when someone close to us is snatched away or when we are forced for other reasons to notice the markers of existence.

Then a feeling of loneliness arises. Many long for a universe that is not cold and indifferent, where the starry heavens do not ignore us, where there is someone – outside our own human boundaries – who observes our wandering progress with tenderness. Sometimes we conduct long discussions late into the night, read thick books, light candles and listen to Brahms. Nevertheless – there is emptiness.

In that case – according to the icon theologians – it could be an idea to visit another source. Where one is seen rather than that one understands. Perhaps we can place the Old Testament's Hagar against the Greeks' Narcissus. Hagar, the single, deserted mother, is driven out into the desert. At the same time she becomes the first person in the Bible who gives a name to God. She says simply:'You are the God who sees and I did not know it.' And she says it next to a spring. Narcissus also looks at himself in a spring but sees only himself. He falls in love with his own mirror image and drowns. The lonely Hagar in the desert drinks from another spring convinced that she is seen by someone who exists outside herself; the only one who sees everything, is capable of everything and bears everything.

And, as we know: the word for 'look' is the same as the word for 'spring' in Hebrew – *'ain.*

The Grand Canal in December rain

God does not 'exist'. I believe in him.

Were he to 'exist' he would be imprisoned in language and consequently our slave.

Were we to 'exist' we would be imprisoned in our language. And so we are, too.

As soon as I turn my dwarfish eyes to God, trying to define Him, he disappears becoming manifest everywhere he is not. His absence is the prerequisite for his existence. One can go on like this and I do.

And I detest those who do not believe in God. There is enough emptiness in me for roses to wither. Enough screams to make the nights to burst. Enough desire to allow myself to be killed in war.

But without God so many words must die: those that no longer find a footing.

Göran Tunström, from *The Christmas Oratorio*

Another evening the cold is penetrating and the rain becomes more intense. The slow journey of the vaporetto through the night becomes a journey of continuous thought through the subconscious. I am reading Joseph Brodsky's words: 'On both sides, knee-deep in pitch black water, stood the enormous carved chests of dark palazzo filled with unfathomable treasures – most likely gold, judging from the low intensity yellow electric glow emerging now and then from cracks in the shutters. Then the sky darkens within the enormous marble parenthesis of a bridge and suddenly everything is bathed in light, the Rialto.' That's exactly how it is.

We pass the palace Ca' d'Oro – this is perhaps the most dazzling of all the palaces; red, gold and blue. This golden house is built in a fantastic Gothic style, fashionable in the fifteenth century, a severe statement of form. A bit further on stands Palazzo Dario, one of the most beautiful in Venice. It is slightly irregular and looks as if it could fall down at any moment.

Before I took the vaporetto I was in the church of Santa Maria degli Scalzi, sometimes called Santa Maria di

Nasareth. Locally it is just called *scalzi* which means barefoot. It is situated only a few metres from the railway station. The church is dedicated to the Spanish mystic John of the Cross (1542–1591) who restarted the discalced Carmelite order, and also to St Teresa of Avila (1515–1582). St John of the Cross, whose statue stands just inside the entrance of the church, talked about negative theology; on darkness as a way to the divine. When I look out over the city I think of how the mystics have traditionally emphasized the necessity of allowing oneself to be led into an inner night, and ignoring one's own feelings. They speak about the importance of delivering oneself up trustingly to something greater, something secret.

I spent the afternoon out at the Lido, not far from the hotel where Thomas Mann wrote the novel *Death in Venice* (1912). The long beach is deserted. The hotel is empty. This evening I have walked right across the narrow peninsula and have now taken the vaporetto in towards the city. The rain over the city mirrors the cupolas and campanile in the wet stones, in an unforgettable way. In *Watermark*, Joseph Brodsky wrote:

> Still winter is an abstract season; it is low on colours, even in Italy and big on the imperatives of cold and brief daylight. These things train your eye on the outside with intensity greater than that of the electric bulb availing you of your own features in the evening. For this is the city of the eye; your other faculties play a faint second fiddle. The way the hues and rhythms of the local facades try to smooth the waves' ever-changing colours and patterns ... In winter you wake up in this city especially on Sundays, to the chiming of its innumerable bells, as though behind your gauze curtains a gigantic teaset were vibrating on a silver tray in the pearl-grey sky behind floral curtains ... On days like this, the city indeed acquires a porcelain aspect, what with all its zinc covered cupolas resembling teapots or upturned cups, and the tilted profiles of campanile clinking like abandoned spoons melting in the sky.

The city is full of the dark silhouettes of church domes and roofs; bridges which make arches over the curved mass of water, which in both ends are cut off by infinity. I look at Brodsky's text again: 'A few dimly lit boats now and then prowled about disturbing with their propellers the reflection of a large neon CINZANO trying to settle on the black oilcloth of the water's surface.' It cannot be said any better than that. It is like a blinding darkness.

The blinding darkness

'The blinding darkness' is a well-used metaphor in descriptions of the spiritual path. It is mainly used by John of the Cross – he who talks of the night as a way to the divine. The darkness encompasses both the discovery of one side of God's being and a dimension in man's inner life. But above all the talk of darkness expresses a respect for the holy. But how does one explain it?

With the help of images people sometimes try to adapt God to their own limitations. Theologians try to draw the holy through the needle's eye of 'probability' and create a logical system. But like a slippery eel that which should be explained disappears from the explanatory net.

The Early Church speaks of God's *aseitet*, causelessness. He is himself the basis of his existence and therefore always more incomprehensible than all attributes. He is 'always greater' (*semper major*). Every attempt to capture God finally in philosophical, literary or artistic forms is therefore condemned to failure. One must be content with the analogy: As it is the 'completely immeasurable' that one wishes to depict, one is forced to say something which at the same time is unsayable. One can therefore only speak about what God *is not*; the un-knowable, the in-expressible, the un-dying, the im-measurable or the un-ending. I think of Edith Södergran's yearning: 'I long for the land that is not, for everything that is, I am weary of craving' from *The Country that is not*, translated by Keith Bosley.

In the tradition of the mystics, God is greater than all images. Language is always mistrusted. It is instead through the 'negative' assertions about God – when man mediates on His ineffability – that his soul is led towards God. In this tradition there is a distrust of everyone who maintains that they have captured God in clear formulae. The icon creates a balance between the unspoken and the spoken. It houses the non-explicable. Another way of rising above the boundaries of language is to use contradictions. 'The blinding darkness' is one of these.

The necessity of paradox
All Christian belief balances on the knife edge between the revealed and the concealed. Contradictions lose their power if they are explained by know-it-all exegesis. There are many: God is both revealed *and* hidden. Christ is both true God *and* true man. The believers live *in* the world but are not *of* the world. God can both be understood *and* not understood. In the letter to the Hebrews the paradox of seeing is clear: 'for he was resolute as one who saw the invisible God'. The power of divine secrets moves on another plane than that of thought feelings or will.

There is no logical matter of course in this inner journey. It is not built on the human power of thought. Neither is it based on a theory which is developed to be able to explain the world, human beings or God. The journey is a consequence of a meeting and a dialogue with the Christ who is *at one and the same time* both personal and completely inscrutable.

Or to speak in the dialect of the Carmelite tradition: To meet God is not to hug the teddy bear of one's childhood or to shout 'At last!' when one discovers the meaning of life. God is neither a declaration of principle nor a comfort for the meaninglessness of life. He is the totally different. The Christian life remains a folly for those who do not believe. No-one can explain it to anyone else. The only thing they can do is to show the way, create an inquisitiveness.

The dark passageway
Just as we are riding at anchor and have left the Lido behind us, and can see Venice's cemetery in front, for some

unknown reason the engine stops. It is now pouring with rain and it is icy cold. This is not exactly a Nordic drizzle. The vaporetto is silent and the electricity goes off, only the red and blue warning signals remain on the sides of the boat. The crew speaks into the telephone and then says that there is no problem. Someone is on the way to collect us. We bob silently at anchor; I once again wind my scarf a few extra turns around my neck, put up my hood and stand outside under cover. The moon could be seen recently but it has now disappeared behind the scattering of clouds. The water runs down my face when I go forwards onto the deck. The captain bawls into his telephone. There are only a few passengers amongst us who look across at the dark city. A watery light streams from it.

The mystics say that there is an emptiness which is filled with presence, a silence which is filled with sound, a darkness which is brimming with light. Every person who wishes to realize the inner journey is led carefully or abruptly, sooner or later, into such darkness. Only in this darkness can a person understand not only that God exists, but who He is. Then the normal senses are not enough. One can either build on one's intellectual abilities, one's moral stature, one's unselfish deeds or the comfort of one's feelings. In the dark night God is at work.

Lars Gyllensten writes in *Skuggans återkomst eller Don Juan går igen* (*The return of the Shadow or Don Juan walks again*)

> Perhaps despair is an instrument in the service of external powers, a tool with which his life, or the part of his life over which he himself has no control, works on him in order to bring him to insight ... Perhaps the despair is a mentor in the service of these externanl powers forcing him forwards towards understanding, so that he will stand naked, and stripped of those seductive and miserable costumes and masks with which people hide behind in order to create for themselves their own flattering and bragging illusory world so that they can exchange this world of illusion and lies for the world which they themselves have not created and cannot control.

And I read and try to soften the harsh language of the mystics. Perhaps it should sound like this: When you want to meet yourself it is painful. You must get rid of your external ego. Then something within you is forced to die. This is a painful process. But if you allow this to happen, something else emerges which you were hitherto unaware of.

Only in surrendering yourself at every level – that which the mystical tradition calls the 'Death of the Ego' – do unexpected insights arise of a spiritual reality. Mankind can then be reached there by a sense of the Other. By letting go – surrender – one becomes aware of permanence. God works from within – not through external power or success – but through compassion and sacrifice. This does not mean intellectual sluggishness, nor that people should submit to pious pronouncements in blind obedience. But it speaks of a spiritual reality. In order to see this clearly one is led sooner or later through a 'narrow gate', a dimly lit gate, a dark tunnel. Ylva Eggehorn talks of man being on the way towards an unlit harbour.

The person who not only 'reads about religion' or has a 'spiritual interest' (something which the mystics constantly warn against) but instead lets himself go, who does not just discuss the religious myths or the plausibility of life's questions, but strives for a living dialogue with Christ – something happens to that person. He is led along a path which leads towards insight into the fire in the darkness, a blinding flame.

During the night a person experiences something which breaks into their own lives in *a completely different way* from what they expected. God is experienced as an independent force arising from their own fantasies. Subject and object have changed places. Now the central point is no longer man's perception but God's call. A person is no longer the one who sees but the one who is seen. I think again of the icon in my pocket.

The radical silence is a part of God's way of making Himself known and inescapable. In the darkness of the night the flame of longing shines. I call to mind the prayer of St Augustine: 'Think Lord, that my thirst for you is your own work.'

On the importance of keeping secrets

A destination of the inner journey is described extremely briefly. It is as if the mystics defended themselves – but the point is that one has now come home to oneself within oneself.

The basic advice of the mystics is this: when the perception turns into calm trust – *keep silent*. If I could make a simple paraphrase of their spiritual counsel it would appear banal: Speak quietly of your experiences! Do not try to describe in words what you have experienced. Instead, seek all the more the non-vocal forms for your worship. Go frequently into a church and linger there. Think of nothing. Do not pray. Do not ask for anything but instead stand quite still in front of an icon. Wander slowly around a cemetery or a park.

Even more concretely one could perhaps summarize the mystics' advice like this: When you have made the decision to not only reflect about God but to actively seek Him, there is a basic rule: Do not broadcast your decision far and wide. Instead keep your lips tightly closed on the subject of your secret! You now have to fight an invisible battle. Do not divulge from the beginning your decision to live in the imitation of Christ. That is a matter between you and God and only between the two of you, with the exception of a single, trusted friend.

To keep silent about one's inner life is essential, especially in the beginning. All inflated talk about inner experiences gives nourishment to self-absorption or self-pity. Through silence the trust grows to the one who sees into the concealed. By remaining silent you become accustomed to speaking to the one who hears without words.

Therefore let few people notice what you are doing. Seek as little attention as possible. Only if you are asked can you say anything. *Hint* rather, at what you experience, quietly, firmly and without exaggeration. There is an objectivity which speaks much more powerfully than great words. Soon enough it will become apparent that your secret wakes other people's interest.

The person who carries around a secret is always discovered even without realizing it themselves. They brood on an inner stability which is noticed. Therefore if anyone asks you, then is the time to speak out. Do it inwardly and in small portions. But say nothing except what you have experienced of God's work, even if it is only his absence or his occasional consolation. Deflect away from yourself the whole time and speak about God in small letters. Above all do not speak about spirituality. Ignore religious or ecclesiastical gossip and learn how to harbour confidence in deep silence!

According to the mystics, a person should therefore, paradoxically enough, ignore his own inner life. Instead they would say: Give of yourself, your time and your interests simply and artlessly to others around you. Hint at the reason of your inner peace – but only gradually! This advice of the mystics is hard to swallow, I think. At the same time it is telling in all its brutality.

∾୭୧∾

After waiting for a while we have got a tow and have reached St Mark's Square. The rain has begun to ease off. Soon I will take a vaporetto to Ferrovia for my journey home the following day. Soon everything will return to normal. But on this cold winter evening I am sitting for a while in the Caffè Florian. The man playing the grand piano seems undeterred by the fact that the instrument has become out of tune in the damp. Unembarrassed, false notes sound out over the square. Late evening in Venice turns into a dark night. The wet stones mirror the weak lanterns of the gondolas and the light from the churches. Yes, the darkness here is indeed blinding.

To travel towards the source – a kind of summing up
Later that night I return to Mestre. Cars are thundering past outside. Outside the station tourists are shouting to each other. The rain has stopped and I go into a restaurant for something to eat. I feel completely washed out as I go up the

steps of the hotel and throw myself onto the bed. Tomorrow morning I must drive north. I put my small laptop away and think that it is about time to create some sort of summary.

To put it rather grandly, the journey that I have touched upon has gone from psychology in Rome, through aesthetics in Paris to ethics and religion in Venice. In this way I have attempted to touch on three inner 'stages'. Sometimes the inner journey takes place in this order, but certainly not always. Other processes blend with one another. The background is as follows:

Everybody is sooner or later forced to take stock of their lives to determine their position. It is because of their own actions or those of others that permanently busy people remain in a state of movement and feel rootless. In the end they realize that they are just being blown by the wind. A prerequisite for a change of course is that they take note of where they are and pause. Only then can they take a good look at their lives. For this, the quiet conversations between friends are just as central as keeping a diary or in some other way looking at their lives in context and understanding their own life histories. When a person is listened to and they themselves listen to others their own personalities become clearer. Only in this way can their identities be developed. Only if they have a well-defined core can they develop genuine relationships with others. They should neither be afraid of intimacy nor cling too much to other people.

If a person only focuses on themselves they risk becoming egocentric and self-absorbed. Similarly, someone who never pauses to understand both their own responsibilities and their reliance on others, can barely progress further. We can perhaps call this the psychological period; interest is geared towards learning to know oneself, one's own life story and one's relationships with others. Together, these three factors – recognition of where one is, friendship and integrity – are a *first* step on the inward journey.

What happens after this? Well, if a person stops running round in ever-decreasing circles without taking stock of their lives, then what happens? Then they will often say that yes, they have lived but for what and in what way? Their sights are now turned away from their own self-fulfilment. When work becomes monotonous and emptiness becomes tangible, they seek nourishment. It is now that they seek more lasting values rather than those things that quickly perish. They often (re)discover the treasures of culture. A *second* stage in the inner journey is taken when someone actively searches for the source which can quench this inner thirst. For an innumerable number of people culture, nature and the beauty of music and literature open a door into a sort of alternative reality. The shivers and feelings of deep contentment that can arise during a concert or when they read something that moves them sometimes gives 'hints' of something outside human experience. Joseph Brodsky maintains that 'aesthetics are the mother of ethics' and Fyodor Dostoevsky posits the theory that it is beauty that will save the world.

But in what sense can one say that these unseen worlds actually exist? One part of the Christian mystical tradition maintains that beauty points beyond itself to something deeper and is a manifestation of an unseen reality. The bitter sweet pain – the holy tears – arises because they are memories and reminders of eternity. This however is a threatening statement for a strict materialist, used to inclining towards science and proved experience. Surely Art is in itself quiescent and does not need any religious interpretation? But a philosophical tradition that goes right back to Plato states that the 'form' of beauty 'exists' independently of manifestations and is just as real as the tangible world and that it is indestructible.

But beyond aesthetics further stages have been described. These concern ethics and spirituality. I call this the *third* stage in the meeting between the seen and the unseen. It partly means that human beings – with the greatest respect and with compassion – engage themselves with the needs of their fellow human beings and give of themselves. We can perhaps call our fellow human beings the factual Other. Human beings can also approach the Inscrutable Other –

God. If they take a step beyond themselves and their own experiences they discover that they are moved by something or someone that lies *outside* their own control. The main focus is inserted into the Christian tradition from mankind's own search for the glance of the Other – the eyes of the icon. The sense of the holy is transformed into the meeting with the holy.

Either as a slow realization or more suddenly, many people experience coming into contact with the secret 'Thou'. It is in the meeting with this Face that people rediscover their genuine 'I', the centre which lies inside the social role that they are playing. In order for this relationship to become a real experience the glance is central. People have been transported towards their own and existence's innermost source, the holy Face. (Martin Buber's 'I, Thou')

But then I think to myself: How can one take this final step? Is mankind's longing for the 'kingdom which is not of this world' just an expression of our own ability to fantasise, a ceaseless tendency to create lies about our lives or is it the opposite, an expression of longed for reality? Who has the authority to answer?

The following day when I am loading up my car I notice to my astonishment a little spring in the hotel yard, right next to the car park. It is difficult to see the little mirror of water under the ground. Just behind the spring hangs a little icon on the whitewashed wall. It has practically been destroyed after decades in the sun and rain. The hotel proprietor explains that a Ukrainian guest worker who worked here many years ago used to winch up water from the well. The man was an orthodox Christian. When he came back on sweltering July evenings after working out in the lagoon he used to drink his fill from the well. When the cool of the evening came he often used to sit peacefully as the sun went down next to the little plane tree which had been planted next to the well. The plane tree is now a tall tree. Before the man returned home again he put the icon up on the wall. There it hangs still. The glance of the icon and the water of the well – *'ain*.

EPILOGUE

Not yet – an extremely unscientific postscript

Back in Sweden once again and life continues as usual. I've no more journeys planned for a long time. Everyday life's comforting routine. A late evening at the ICA supermarket. After buying a few sweets it catches my eye. On the video stand I see Ben Hur. That means an evening ahead with my feet up watching TV. The film is long. I go out every now and then to grab a sandwich. The sweat drops off the galloping horses. The masses come to blows. Clashing sword and shining armour. Blood gushes forth when blows are struck. Christians are taken away to be tried. The grotesque soul of the entire Roman Empire is filtered through Hollywood's glamorous colours.

In the middle of this raw film there is a scene that stands out. It only lasts a few minutes. In my memory it lasts for an eternity. Palestine in the hot sun. Some people are standing absolutely still surrounding a man. They are moved, wide-eyed. They are paying careful attention to him. But we only see the man from behind. He is turned away from the camera. Someone falls to their knees. He is apparently saying something, but everything is only hinted at.

It is a pale copy of the original film which flickers in front of my eyes as I sit on the sofa. But I have the same feelings that I had when I first saw the film at the cinema several decades ago; I am deeply moved. The film never shows

Jesus's face but only the reactions of those around him; quiet joy and wide-eyed wonder.

Why do I remember it? Perhaps because the scene respects the need for that which is merely hinted at. It relies on the fact that there is strength in that which is not shown. It reminds us of the secret which the smug faithful seem to forget.

Stray thoughts come into my head. If I were to stand in the vicinity of the compassionate centre of the world and of existence, which is how Jesus refers to God in St John's Gospel, I would rather stand right at the back.

'He who is near me is near the fire' – it is written in one of the apocryphal books of the Bible. Fire consumes. The happiness of those who ask in a self-satisfied way: 'How do you feel about faith, dear friend?' makes me thoughtful. Talk of peace and harmony makes me suspicious despite romantic talk about the blinding darkness. I prefer to believe in the flames, the all-consuming. I prefer provocation, the all-transforming. One has to duck down before it, hide oneself and look away. Who am I to look the world's Saviour in the eye?

Cute pictures of Jesus in bright modern churches with colourful carpets and coffee and biscuits make me nervous. Especially if the pictures are colourful and the young people sway as they sing 'Alleluia' with uplifted arms. Then I want to leave. Stylized icons suit me better; they never try to be personal. But I prefer to stand right at the back of a dark church.

It is the thought of the icon's living gaze – directed at me personally – that I find difficult to cope with. I am happy for others to formulate the correct belief. I find it easier to recognize myself as the one who said: 'Go away from me. I am a sinful man', than to discuss the philosophy of life, the Desert Fathers or ecumenism. I find it easier to be comforted by the rejected Jesus, 'He was as one from whom one hides one's face', than to creep up into Mary's arms. The dead Jesus; the artist Holbein's dead Jesus – he who is lying with his sunken breast on the ground after he has been

taken down from the Cross – I can gaze on him for a long
time. I saw the picture in the Dostoevsky Museum in St
Petersburg. Dostoevsky was bewitched when he saw it for
the first time in Basle. When I look at it I think: it was for
me that He died and it is with me that He will die. But the
living gaze directed at me. No – not yet. The cause of this
respect? I feel – and some times experience – that existence
has a centre in this man. In his kingdom absolute love reigns
– not tepidity. And before this absolute my own laxity
stands out in relief. Like a fool I mostly believe that he was
born, lived, died, rose from the dead and still lives in the
midst of a bewildered Christendom. Furthermore I believe
quite impudently that he is unique. Not because it is reason-
able or because it is written in a book but because I rely on
God's own way of making himself known; in a historical
figure, in degradation, in the folly of compassion.

Yes of course, I know! There are myriads of saviour
figures in the millennium's mystical torrent. In Japan alone
there are a thousand religions. Despite this, or perhaps
because of this, I often have a raw and simple belief that
God – this beyond-human figure, mighty in a nucleus of
compassion – chose a specific person in a specific culture so
that he could through him (quietly but determinedly) bring
mankind's attention to his existence and will. This is a
confession of foolishness and the absurd, of a scandal. This
is a confession that the cosmos is not just here by accident,
that people's lives are not a meaningless hotchpotch of
memory fragments. A quiet joy. There is Someone who
desires us.

But the thought that there is in fact a living God is practically terrifying in its sacred exploding euphoria. I hardly
dare write the words. When I touch on the meaning of the
thought that we are not alone, that death has been
vanquished, that our guilt has been removed, that evil will
not triumph, I notice within myself a mixture of trembling
joy and unspeakable – yes exactly, un-speakable – gratitude. If God has entered into our existence through the man
in the icon, then the fear of emptiness, the loathing of life's

transience which is apparently not easily dealt with and our disquiet about the future and death are completely unjustified. The compass needle has stopped spinning. Existence is not just chance. But neither are we locked into some divine plan. There is a Friend, the ultimate friend whom we shall one day see face to face. But not yet – no, not yet.

∾❀∾

It is my job to seek answers to unanswerable questions – empirically and logically. Research has its time. All unanswerable 'whys?' I twist and turn constantly, but finally I lay them quietly in a pile because I have a feeling – which borders on certainty – that the man in the icon is the one who is the world's starting point and goal; the Saviour and Comforter of the whole world and of me personally. It sounds bombastic and it *is* folly. But folly should be anchored in its correct place, and not applied to religious cliché or banality but to the radicalism in the contents of the icon.

So what were the arguments again? I haven't so many rational arguments. Intellectually it appears just as probable that the world is lacking in gods. But I have a sort of reliance on the icon's gaze. This belief is not controllable or replicable. It is existential. If one first takes note of what the man maintained about Himself and then in great simplicity try to follow what he said (this is called the Imitation of Christ), small but distinct signs appear along the way. The things that he talked about do not just appear as fantasy. The kingdom of God is within us all – even if only as something longed for. What was it that Gunnar Ekelöf wrote? 'Eternity exists because we lack it. No-one need be afraid:' 'Sometimes two times two is not four but five', says Fyodor Dostoevsky.

Yes, of course, I know all the counter-arguments. It is my job to point them out. But at the same time I am convinced that it is neither logic nor science that leads us to believe. It is merely the astonishment that we have been invited, although unworthy, to be close to the core of the universe. The astonishment that this unreserved love, which has sacrificed itself, applies solely to us and for all eternity sounds pretentious or conceited. But that is obviously how it is. Brooding on this secret I go – like all other people who are fascinated by the man in the icon – through the world as if in a grandiose cipher. I sense a hand in great events as well as small. Existence rests in an intention – a glance, existence is re-centred, has a hub. Our life's journey has a harbour – face to face.

I stuff my hand into my pocket and make sure that the icon is still there. I take it out and put it on the coffee table. The same inscrutable look. The more the years pass, the less impressed I am by cultivated intellectual brilliance. Research is a qualified and conscious method of limiting existence to given perspectives and methods. Without knowledge and critical thought, existence would be constricted. But the overview – the big enigmas – what do we do with them, friends?

External appearances seem just as unimportant as great learning or sharp intellects. Sight fades away. Life slides slowly downhill. Even my life's journey will come to an end. Even more I feel compassion for all those whose intellectual honesty means that they cannot acknowledge their own longing to return home. I feel as if I am standing gazing at the back of Ben Hur's Jesus figure and observing all those who are fascinated by his face. In several years he will turn round and look at me. Living I would not be able to withstand his glance. I would die of happiness. That I do not want to do. Just yet.

BIBLIOGRAPHY

Books in English or English translation

Bauman, Z., *From Pilgrim to tourist: A short history of identity*, London, Saga Publications, 1996.

Bauman, Z., *Globalization: the human consequences*, London, Polity Press, 1998.

Bauman, Z., *Liquid Love. On the frailty of human bonds*, Cambridge, Polity Press, 2003.

Berger, J., *Ways of seeing*, BBC Publications, London, Penguin Books, 1982.

Berman, M., *All that is solid melts into air. The experience of modernity*, London and New York, Verso, 1983.

Blackden, P., *Danger down under*, London, Virgin Books, 2002.

Blackden, P., *Tourist trap. When holiday turns to nightmare*, London, Virgin Books, 2003.

Botton, A. de, *The consolations of philosophy*, New York, Pantheon Books, 2001.

Botton, A. de, *The art of travel*, New York, Panthen Books, 2002.

Brodsky, J., *Less than one. Selected Essays*, New York, Farrar, Straus & Giroux, 1987.

Brodsky, J., *Watermark*, London, Penguin Books, 1992.

Brodsky, J., *Religious Ethics. A theological study of making and meaning*, Princeton, Princeton University Press, 1989.

Butler, R. W. and Pearce, D. G. (eds), *Change to tourism. People, places, processes*, London, Routledge, 1995.

Carter, W., *Marcel Proust: A life*, London/New Haven, Yale University Press, 2000.

Cohen, E., *A Phenomenology of Tourist experiences*. I: Apostolopoulos, Y., et al., *The sociology of tourism*, London, Routledge, 1996.

Ekelöf, Gunnar, 'Diwan over the Prince of Emgion', in *Selected Poems*, W. H. Auden and Leif Sjöberg (trs), New York, Pantheon Books, 1971.

Elsrud, T., *Risk creation in travelling. Backpackers adventure narration. Annals of tourism research*, vol. 28, issue 3, National University of Singapore, Singapore Tourist Board, 2001, pp. 597–617.

Featherstone, M., *Consumer culture and postmodernism*, London, Sage Publications, 1991.

Gustafsson, L. *Elegies and other poems*, tr. Christopher Middleton and Yvonne L. Sandström, New York, A New Directions Book, 1996.

Houellebecq, M., *Platform*, London, Heinemann, 2002.

Kaplan, R. and Kaplan, S., *The experience of nature. A psychological perspective*, Cambridge, Cambridge University Press, 1989.

Kolakowski, L., *Religion: If there is no God*, London, Fontana Press, 1983.

Leclercq, J., *The love of learning and the desire for God. A study of monastic culture*, London, SPCK, 1978.

Löfgren, O., *On holiday. A history of vacationing*, Berkeley, University of California Press, 1999.

Mann, T. *Death in Venice*, tr. Michal Henry Heim, Harper-Collins, New York, 2004.

McDowell, L. (ed.), *Undoing place. A geographical reader*, London, Arnold, 1997.

O'Dell, T. (ed.), *Nonstop*, Lund University, 1999.

Pelton, R. Young, *Fielding's The world's most dangerous places*, Rendondo Beach, Fielding Worldwide, 1998.

Powys, J. C., *A philosophy of solitude*, London, Jonathan Cape, 1933.

Powys, J. C., *The Art of Happiness*, W. W. Norton & Co. Inc., New York, 1937.

Powys, J. C., *The meaning of culture*, W. W. Norton & Co. Inc., New York, 1929, 1957.

Proust M., *In search of lost time. 1 The Way by Swann's*, tr. Lydia Davis, London, Penguin Books, 2002.

Relph, E., *Place and placelessness*, London, Pion, 1976.

Rojek, C., *Decentering leisure*, London, Sage, 1995.

Seneca, L. Annaeus, *Letters from a Stoic*, London, Penguin Classics, 1969.

Seneca, L. Annaeus, *On the Shortness of Life*, tr. C. D. N. Costa, Penguin Books, Great Ideas, 1997.

Sidenap, G., *The variety of ineffability*, New York, Stahlberg Press, 2003.

Tranströmer. T., *New Collected Poems*, tr. Robin Fulton, Tarset, Northumberland, Boodaxe Books, 1997.

Tunström, G., *The Christmas Oratorio*, tr. Paul Hoover, Lincoln Massachusets, David R. Godine, 1995.

Urry, J., *The tourist gaze. Leisure and travel in contemporary societies*, London, Sage Publications, 1990.

Urry, J. and Rojek, C. (eds), *Touring cultures: transformations of travel and theory*, London, Routledge, 2001.

Yalom, I., *Existential Psychotherapy*, London, Basic Books, 1980.

Books published in Swedish and other languages

Alberoni, F., *L'Amicizia*, Milan, Garzanti, 1987.

Berg-Eriksen, T., *Augustin. Det urulige hjertet*, Oslo, Universitetsforlaget, 2001.

Bergman, S., *I begynnelsen är bilden. En befriende bildkonst-kultur-teologi*, Stockholm, Proprius, 2003.

Bjerg, S., *Synets teologi*, Fredriksberg, Anis, 1999.

Bodin, P. A., *Världen som ikon. Åtta föredrag om den ryskortodoxa andliga traditionen*, Skellefteå, Artos & Normas-förlag, 1987.

Bruhn, J. and Rasmussen, B., *Proust: En modern introduktion till På spaning efter den tid som flytt*, Kågeröd, Barrs bokförlag, 2000.

Cederholm, E. Andersson, *Det extaordinarie lockelse.* *Luffarturistens bilder och upplevelser,* Lund, Arkiv förlag, 1991, Avhandlingsserie 51.

Dalman, J. F., *Guds tilltal i det sköna,* Uppsala, Teologiska institutionen, 1989.

Daun, Å., *Svenskt mentalitet,* 3 edns, Stockholm, Raben Prisma, 1998.

Englund, P., *Tystnadens historia och andra essayer,* Stockholm, Atlantis, 2003.

Eriksen, T. Hylland, *Ögonblickets tyrrani. Snabb och långsam tid i informationssamhället,* Nora, Nya Doxa, 2001.

Eskilsson, L. and Fazlhashemi, M. (eds), *Reseberättelser. Idéhistoriska resor i sociala och geografiska rum,* Stockholm, Carlsson, 2001.

Fakta om svensk turism, Stockholm, Turistdelegationen, 2003.

Frändberg, L., *'Fritidens globalisering ur ett rörlighetsperspectiv. Enkunskats översikt',* FBG rapport, 31, 2000.

Granqvist, R. (ed.), *Villfarelsens blick. Essayer om resan som kultur,* Stockholm Stehag, Brutus Östlings bokförlag Symposium, 1996.

Gyllensten, L., *Skuggans återkomst eller Don Juan går igen,* Stockholm, Bonniers, 1985.

Hagelin, G., *Alla tiders Rom,* Stockholm, Verbum, 1971.

Hansen, K. and Salmonsson, K. (eds), *Fönster mot Europa: Platser och identiteter,* Lund, Lund Studentlitteratur, 2001.

Herlitz, G., *Svenskar hur vi är och varför,* Uppsala Publishing House, 2003.

Hermansson, L., *Gå till gå,* Stockholm, Bokförlaget Lejd, 2000.

Holmqvist, S. and Mathlein, A. (eds), *Resande mål. Svenska författare med aptit på världen,* Stockholm, Carlsson, 2000.

Hylinger, C., *'Om Prousts humor',* eds I: Hjort, Maris and Svensson, Ingrid, *Om Proust,* Enskede, Marcel Proust sällskapet, 1996.

Johanisson, K., *Nostalgia. En känslas historia. Stockholm*, Bonnier essä, 2001.

Jonsson, G., *'Rotad, rotlös och rastlös. Ung mobilitet i tid och rum'*, Kulturgeografi GERUM 3, Umeå, Umeå University, 2003.

Kalvemark, T., *Låset av ull. Utsikter över andliga landskap*, Skellefteå, Norma, 2001.

Kaminski, M., *Venedig. Konst och arkitektur*, Cologne, Konemann, 2001.

Karnborg, U., *Stjärnfältet. En essai om helgon och skostav*. Stockholm, Bonnier, 2003.

Kjaerstad, J., *Forforaren*, Stockholm, Atlantis, 1997.

Kjaerstad, J., *Erovraren*, Stockholm, Atlantis, 1998.

Kjaerstad, J. , *Upptäckaren*, Stockholm, Atlantis, 2001.

Krogh, G., *Tankar om ikonen*, Stockholm, Artos & Norma, 2004.

Kyrklund, W., *Prosa*, Stockholm, Bonnier Alba, 1995.

Lossky, V., *Östkyrkans mystiska teologi*, Skellefteå, Artos, 1997. Original title: *La thëoligie mystique de l'église d'Orient*.

Löfgren, O., *'Längtan till landet Annorlunda. Om turism i historia och nutid'*, Stockholm, Gidlund/Sveriges Turistråd, 1990.

Löfström, T., *Mannen som reste och 47 andra reseberättelser*, Stockholm, Vagabond, 2000.

Magris, C., *Donau*, Stockholm, Forum, 1990. Original title: *Danubia*.

Martinson, H., *Resor utan mål*, Stockholm, Bonniers, 1943.

Martinson, H., *Aniara*, Albert Bonniers förlag, Stockholm, 1956.

Oddner, F., *Kafékultur, kommunikation och gränser*, Akademiska avhandling, Lund, Sociologiska institutionen, 2003.

Proust, M., *På spaning efter den tid som flytt V Den fångna*, Stockholm, Natur och Kultur, 1983. Original title: *La Prisonniere*.

På resande fot, 23 forskare skriver om turism och

upplevelser. Stockholm, Sellin & Partner, 2001.

Ramqvist, K., 'Den globala terapin', *Arena*, no. 3, Stockholm, Premiss, 2003.

Sadolin, E., *På vandring i Venedig*, Stockholm, Gebers, 1957.

SAS, *Ungdomers resedrömmar*, Stockholm, 2002.

Sigurdsson, O., *Hungerns väg*, Lund, Arcus, 2000.

Sundbärg, G., *Det svenska folklynnet*, Stockholm, Norstedts, 1911.

Svedelid, O., *Reseliv*, Stockholm, Sellin & Partner, 2000.

Wikström, O., *Det bländande mörkret. Om psykologi och andlig vägledning i vår tid*, Örebro, Libris, 2001.

Wikström, O., *Långsamhetens lov eller vådan av att åka moped genom Louvren*, Stockholm, Natur och Kultur, 2001.

Wikström, O., *Om heligheten och dess envisa vägran att försvinna*, Stockholm, Natur och Kultur, 2003a.

Wikström, O., 'Musik och mystik hos Marcel Proust – religionspsykologiska perspectiv på litterära texter', I: Bråkenhielm, C. R. & Pettersson, T. (eds), *Att fånga världen i ord. Litteratur och livsåskådning*, Skellefteå, Norma, 2003b.

Wikström, O., *En liten vägledning till nåden*, Örebro, Cordia, 2004.

Wolf, E., *Med charter till Estoril. En etnologisk studie av kulturell mångfald inom modern svensk turism*, Skrifter från etnologiska föreningen i Västsverige, 2001, 3:33.

Ziehe, L., *Kulturanalyser: ungdomer, utbildning, modernitet. Essäer*. Smnst, J. Fornäs & J Retzlaff, Stockholm-Stehag. Symposium, 1989.

Ålund, A, *Multikultiungdom: Kön, etnicitet, identitet*, Lund, Studentlitteratur, 1997.

www.ingramcontent.com/pod-product-compliance
Lightning Source LLC
LaVergne TN
LVHW051519080426
835509LV00017B/2112